MW00892365

VISITING COSTA RICA

Discovering Unexplored Treasure, Tourist
Attraction, and Historical Wealth of Costa
Rica (Travel Guide)

OLIVAR ANDY

Copyright © 2024 by Olivar Andy

All rights reserved. No part of this publication may be reproduced, distributed, or transmitted in any form or by any means, including photocopying, recording, or other electronic or mechanical methods, without the prior written permission of the publisher, except in the case of brief quotations embodied in critical reviews and certain other noncommercial uses permitted by copyright law.

For permission requests, contact the publisher.

Disclaimer ⚠

The information provided in this "Costa Rica Travel Guide" is accurate to the best of the author's knowledge and experience at the time of publication. However, the author and publisher make no representation or warranties with respect to the accuracy or completeness of the contents of this guidebook and specifically disclaim any implied warranties of merchantability or fitness for a particular purpose. The author and publisher shall have no liability to any person or entity with respect to any loss or damage caused or alleged to be caused directly or indirectly by the information contained in this guidebook.

Table of Contents

Map of Costa Rica

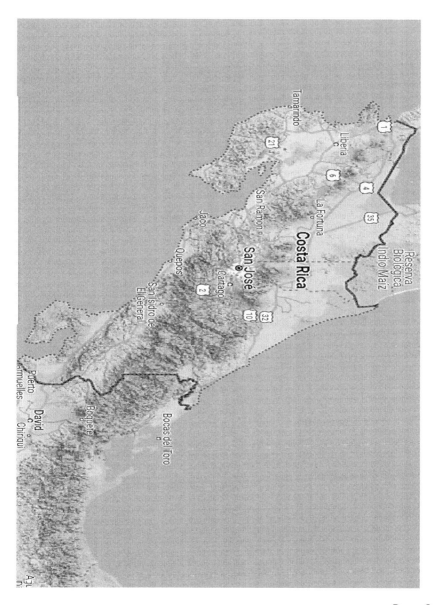

WELCOME TO COSTA RICA

A WARM INTRODUCTION

Welcome, dear traveler, to the vibrant and lush land of Costa Rica! As you begin on this voyage, you will discover a world where nature's abundance is on full show, residents greet you with a passionate "Pura Vida," and every turn offers an adventure.

Costa Rica, a treasure set between the Pacific Ocean and the Caribbean Sea, is a haven for travelers seeking both peace and adventure. Here, you'll discover beautiful jungles alive with unique fauna, stunning beaches caressed by turquoise waves, and volcanoes that watch over the landscape.

But Costa Rica is much than simply its picture-perfect scenery. It is a country with a rich history, a diverse population, and a dedication to conservation that has made it a leader in sustainable tourism. As you explore this wonderful country, you'll discover stories of past civilizations, meet a varied cast of characters, and see firsthand the attempts to preserve this paradise for future generations.

For you, the first-time tourist, this guide will help you discover Costa Rica's attractions. Costa Rica has something for everyone, whether you're an adrenaline junkie looking to zip-line through the canopy, a nature lover hoping to sight a majestic quetzal, or a beachcomber seeking the peace and quiet of a remote cove.

So pack your luggage, bring your spirit of adventure, and get ready to fall in love with Costa Rica. Your adventure is about to begin, and we are here to help you every step of the way. Welcome to the Land of Pura Vida!

Meet the Author: Your Travel Companion

Hello, fellow traveler! I'm Olivar Andy, your guide and companion on this fantastic adventure through the heart of Costa Rica. As a traveler and writer, I've spent years discovering the nooks and corners of this lovely country, and I'm excited to share my experiences and ideas with you.

My love of travel began at an early age and has led me all around the world. However, Costa Rica has a particular place in my heart. It's a place that never ceases to astonish me, no matter how often I return. From the moment I stepped foot on its soil, I was enthralled by its natural beauty, rich culture, and welcoming people.

Over the years, I've hiked through its jungles, ridden its waves, and enjoyed its gastronomic marvels. I've danced with the natives at exuberant fiestas, marveled at the fauna, and found consolation in the peaceful scenery. Each visit has been a fresh journey, and I've gained a wealth of knowledge, tales, and hidden jewels along the way.

In this book, my goal is to be more than simply an author; I want to be your travel buddy. I'll be there for you every step of the way, from organizing your vacation to enjoying the final moments of your Costa Rican journey. My objective is to help you make wonderful moments, discover the beauty of Pura Vida, and experience Costa Rica in the same way that I did: with amazement, pleasure, and an open heart.

So let us go on this trip together. With this book in hand and an adventurous attitude in your heart, you're ready to discover Costa Rica's delights. Welcome aboard, and let the journey begin!

Navigating This Guide: Tips for First-Timers

Welcome to the ideal travel companion for visiting Costa Rica! If you're new to the world of travel guides, don't worry. Here are some recommendations to help you easily explore this book and get the most out of your Costa Rican adventure:

Start with the basics: Start by reading the introductory parts. These will provide you with an overview of what to anticipate in Costa Rica, the best times to visit, and important travel recommendations.

Plan Your Journey: Use the area highlights and top attractions chapters to create an itinerary. Consider what interests you the most, whether it's beaches, jungles, animals, or outdoor activities.

Dive Deeper: Each section is intended to give thorough information on a certain topic. For example, the "Beach Bliss" chapter will lead you to the greatest coastal sites, while "Outdoor Thrills" will provide information on adventurous activities.

Customize Your Experience: The "Sample Itineraries" section is a fantastic place to start, but feel free to mix and combine options to design a trip that meets your needs and timeline.

Embrace the Culture: The "Culinary Journey" and "Urban Adventures" chapters will introduce you to local cuisine and city life. Don't miss out on sampling traditional cuisine and touring the colorful towns.

Stay Informed: The "Useful Information" section addresses practical issues such as health and safety, money management, and transportation. Keep this information available for a pleasant and worry-free journey.

Be a Responsible Traveler: The "Traveling Responsibly" chapter explains ways to protect the environment and local communities throughout your trip.

Keep It Handy: Carry this handbook with you when you travel. It is not just a preparation tool, but also a useful resource throughout your journey for rapid reference and on-the-spot judgments.

Make Notes: Feel free to scribble down your own notes, tips, and favorite locations in the guide. It will become a personalized travel notebook and a treasured keepsake of your adventure.

Enjoy the Adventure: Most importantly, follow this guidance to optimize your experience while remembering to welcome the unexpected. The finest travel memories are often the result of spontaneous decisions and unanticipated diversions.

BEFORE YOU GO: PLANNING YOUR ADVENTURE

BEST TIMES TO VISIT: SEASONS AND FESTIVALS

Understanding Costa Rica's climate:

Costa Rica has a tropical climate with two distinct seasons: Verano (dry season) and Invierno (rainy season). The dry season normally lasts from December to April, whereas the  rainy season lasts from May to November. However, the weather might differ by region.

 Dry Season (December-April):
Weather is sunny and dry, with temperatures ranging from 70°F to 90°F (21°C to 32°C).
Ideal for: Beach holidays, animal viewing, and outdoor activities like as hiking and zip-lining.

Popular festivals:
Fiesta de los Diablitos: This event, held in the indigenous town of Boruca in late December or early January, includes traditional masks, dances, and music.

Envision Festival (February/March): A lively festival of music, art, and yoga in Uvita, which draws international tourists.

 Rainy Season (May-November):
Weather: Afternoon rains are prevalent, with beautiful scenery and milder temps.
Best for: Whitewater rafting, waterfall exploration, and admiring the lush environment.

Popular festivals:
Celebration de la Tortuga (September/October): Held in Tortuguero, this celebration commemorates the sea turtle breeding season.
Dia de la Independencia (September 15): A nationwide celebration of Costa Rica's independence with parades and traditional music.

Regional considerations:
Caribbean Coast: The weather is less dependable, with rain possible throughout year but a dry spell in September and October.
Northwest Costa Rica (Guanacaste) is drier than the rest of the nation, having a distinct dry season.

Tips for Selecting the Best Time to Visit:

Consider Your Interests: If you enjoy surfing, the wet season delivers larger waves, particularly along the Pacific coast. For birding, the dry season is optimal.

Festival Fans: Find out when local festivals are held and plan your trip around them.

Budget travelers: Prices for lodgings and tours may be reduced during the wet season, with the exception of July and August, which are popular vacation months for both locals and Europeans.

Crowd Avoidance: If you want to see fewer visitors, go during the shoulder months (May, June, and November), when the weather is a combination of rain and sunlight and the crowds are smaller.

Packing Essentials: What to Bring

Item	Description	Tick Box
Passport & Travel Documents	Valid passport, visas (if required), travel insurance, and itinerary.	■
Clothing	Lightweight, breathable clothing for warm weather.	■
Rain Gear	Waterproof jacket or poncho for the rainy season.	■
Footwear	Comfortable walking shoes, sandals, and water shoes for beaches.	■
Sun Protection	Sunglasses, hat, and high SPF sunscreen.	■
Insect Repellent	DEET-based or natural repellent for mosquitoes.	■

Medications	**Prescription medicines, pain relievers, and anti-diarrheal medication.**	■
First Aid Kit	**Band-aids, antiseptic wipes, and blister pads.**	■
Toiletries	**Toothbrush, toothpaste, shampoo, and other personal hygiene items.**	■
Camera & Binoculars	**For capturing memories and wildlife spotting.**	■
Reusable Water Bottle	**To stay hydrated and reduce plastic waste.**	■
Snacks & Energy Bars	**For quick energy boosts during activities.**	■
Beach Gear	**Swimsuit, beach towel, and snorkeling equipment (if needed).**	■
Eco-Friendly Products	**Biodegradable soap, reef-safe sunscreen, and reusable bags.**	■

Power Adapter & Charger	**For electronic devices, compatible with Costa Rica's outlets (Type A/B).**	■
Flashlight or Headlamp	**Useful for night walks and power outages.**	■
Cash & Credit Cards	**Costa Rican colones and a backup credit card for emergencies.**	■
Travel Guide & Map	**For navigating and exploring Costa Rica.**	■
Spanish Phrasebook	**To communicate basic phrases and questions.**	■
Lightweight Backpack	**For day trips and excursions.**	■

Travel Insurance: Safety First

Travel insurance is a crucial component of your vacation planning, providing peace of mind and protection against unforeseen situations. Here's why it's essential for your Costa Rican journey.

Medical coverage: Costa Rica offers outstanding healthcare services, particularly in the big cities. However, medical treatment might be expensive for travelers. Travel insurance can pay for medical expenditures, emergency evacuation, and hospital stays.

Trip Cancellation and Interruption: Unexpected events, like as harsh weather or illness, might derail your plans. Travel insurance can help you pay for non-refundable charges like flights and hotel reservations.

Lost or Stolen Items: In the event of lost luggage or theft, travel insurance can compensate for personal belongings such as passports and gadgets.

Costa Rica is well-known for its adventure sports, including zip line, surfing, and whitewater rafting. Make sure your coverage covers these hobbies, as some insurance plans exclude high-risk sports.

24/7 Assistance: Most travel insurance packages provide round-the-clock emergency assistance, guiding and assisting you when you need it most.

When purchasing travel insurance, compare multiple companies and study the small print to understand the coverage limitations, exclusions, and deductibles. It's a simple investment that may help you avoid major financial losses and worry throughout your vacation.

Entry Requirements: Passports and Visa

Before traveling to Costa Rica, it is essential to understand the entrance criteria to guarantee a smooth arrival.

Passport: All passengers must have a passport that is valid for at least six months before expiration. Ensure that your passport contains at least one blank page for entrance and departure stamps.

Visa: Many countries, including the United States, Canada, and the majority of European nations, do not require visas for visits of up to 90 days. However, it is important to verify the most recent visa requirements for your nationality on the official website of the Costa Rican embassy or consulate in your country.

Proof of Onward Travel: You may be required to present proof of onward travel, such as a return ticket or a ticket to a place other than Costa Rica.

Proof of Funds: Some passengers may be needed to demonstrate financial soundness, often $100 per month of expected stay.

Health Requirements: Depending on the global health condition, there may be additional health requirements, such as immunizations or COVID-19 rules. Always check the most recent health advisories prior to your journey.

For Costa Map, Click the Link Below or scan the QR Code

COSTA RICA G-MAP

FIRST IMPRESSIONS: UNDERSTANDING COSTA RICA

Geography: From Mountains to Coasts

Costa Rica is a region of outstanding natural beauty, with a diversified landscape that includes towering mountains and lovely coasts. It is located in Central America, bordering Nicaragua to the north, Panama to the southeast, the Pacific Ocean to the west, and the Caribbean Sea to the east. Costa Rica's unusual geographical location has resulted in a diverse range of landscapes and microclimates, making it a paradise for nature lovers and adventurers alike.

Central Valley: Costa Rica's core, which includes the capital city of San José, is set on a plateau surrounded by mountains and volcanoes. This region is the country's cultural and political hub, with a pleasant climate and fertile fields.

Mountain Ranges: Several mountain ranges cross the nation, including the Cordillera de Guanacaste, Cordillera Central, and Cordillera de Talamanca. The mountains are home to both active and extinct volcanoes, including Arenal, Poás, and Irazú, which provide breathtaking views and hot springs.

Costa Rica has more than 1,200 kilometers (745 miles) of coastline, with the Pacific coast famous for its beautiful beaches, surf places, and marine species. The Caribbean shore, on the other hand, has a more relaxed atmosphere, complete with beautiful rainforests, coral reefs, and Afro-Caribbean culture.

Rainforests & National Parks: The country is well-known for its conservation efforts, with over 25% of its territory preserved as national parks and reserves. The Monteverde Cloud Forest Reserve and Corcovado National Park are just two examples of lush ecosystems that sustain a diverse range of animals, including exotic birds and secretive jaguars.

Rivers and waterfalls: Costa Rica's environment is crisscrossed by numerous rivers, ideal for whitewater rafting and kayaking. The La Fortuna Waterfall and Rio Celeste are among the numerous spectacular waterfalls that draw people from all over the world.

A Quick Look at History: Key Moments

Costa Rica's history includes a patchwork of indigenous civilizations, Spanish colonialism, and a peaceful transition to democracy and progress.

During the pre-Columbian era, Costa Rica was home to indigenous communities such the Chorotega, Boruca, and Bribrí. These civilizations lived in peace with nature, depending on agriculture, hunting, and fishing.

Spanish colonialism began when Christopher Columbus arrived on the Caribbean coast in 1502. The region, however, was not as wealthy in gold and silver as other regions of the Americas, resulting in a reliance on agriculture and a tiny colonial population.

Costa Rica achieved independence from Spain in 1821 as a member of the Central American Federation. It became a sovereign nation in 1838, marking the start of its independence as a republic.

Costa Rica dissolved its army in 1948, following a brief civil war. This choice represented the country's dedication to peace and shifted national resources to education, healthcare, and environmental protection.

Environmental Leadership: In the late twentieth and early twenty-first centuries, Costa Rica became a global leader in environmental protection and sustainable development. The government has set lofty targets for renewable energy and aspires to be carbon neutral.

Embracing Pura Vida: The Costa Rican Way

"Pura Vida" is more than simply a word in Costa Rica; it is a concept that encapsulates the country's way of life. Pura Vida, which translates as "pure life" or "simple life," is about enjoying the small things, living life to the fullest, and having a good attitude.

Costa Rica's Pura Vida is evident in its people's warm welcome, emphasis on community and family, and great respect for environment. It's a reminder to slow down, appreciate the present moment, and find delight in life's little pleasures. Pura Vida is a way of life that encourages you to embrace pleasure and fulfillment, whether you're watching a gorgeous sunset, having a leisurely lunch with friends, or simply admiring the beauty of nature.

Pura Vida will be there in your daily encounters and experiences as you travel across Costa Rica. It is reflected in the courteous greetings of inhabitants, the slow pace of life, and the country's dedication to preserve its breathtaking surroundings. Embracing Pura Vida entails cultivating a grateful and thoughtful mentality, and it is a concept that may help you enjoy your time in Costa Rica and beyond.

VISIT COSTA RICA

Language Basics: Essential Spanish Phrases

While many Costa Ricans speak English, especially in tourist areas, knowing some basic Spanish phrases can enhance your travel experience and help you connect with locals. Here's a comprehensive list of essential Spanish phrases for various situations:

Greetings:
Hello: Hola
Good morning: Buenos días
Good afternoon: Buenas tardes
Good evening: Buenas noches
How are you? (formal): ¿Cómo está usted?
How are you? (informal): ¿Cómo estás?
Nice to meet you: Mucho gusto
Goodbye: Adiós

Basic Communication:
Please: Por favor
Thank you: Gracias
You're welcome: De nada
Excuse me: Disculpe
Sorry: Lo siento
Yes: Sí
No: No
I don't understand: No entiendo

Do you speak English? ¿Habla inglés?

Directions and Travel:
Where is...? ¿Dónde está...?
How far is...? ¿A qué distancia está...?
Can you help me? ¿Puede ayudarme?
I'm looking for... Estoy buscando...
Left: Izquierda
Right: Derecha
Straight ahead: Recto
Map: Mapa

Dining and Food:
I'm hungry: Tengo hambre
I'm thirsty: Tengo sed
Menu: Menú
Bill, please: La cuenta, por favor
Water: Agua
Coffee: Café
Beer: Cerveza
Vegetarian: Vegetariano/a

Accommodation:
Hotel: Hotel
Room: Habitación
Reservation: Reserva
Do you have availability? ¿Tiene disponibilidad?

Emergencies:
Help! ¡Ayuda!
Police: Policía
Doctor: Médico
Hospital: Hospital
Pharmacy: Farmacia

EXPLORING THE LAND: REGIONAL HIGHLIGHTS

Central Valley: Heart of the Country

The Central Valley is a mesmerizing location located in the heart of Costa Rica. Here's what you should know:

 Geography and location:

The Central Valley is located in Costa Rica's central highlands, surrounded by beautiful mountain ranges and fertile valleys.

It includes large cities like as San José (the capital), Alajuela, Heredia, and Cartago.

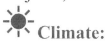 **Climate:**

The Central Valley's climate is delightfully moderate due to its height. Expect colder temperatures than in coastal locations.

The days are warm, but the evenings may be delightfully cold.

Natural Beauty:

The region is defined by its verdant coffee farms, undulating hills, and scenic scenery.

Explore the cloud forests, national parks, and volcanic summits.

🎲 **Activities & Attractions:**

Poás Volcano: Visit the Poás Volcano National Park to see the breathtaking blue crater lake.

La Paz Waterfall Gardens include waterfalls, fauna, and butterfly gardens.

Explore the Orosi Valley, which features colonial churches and hot springs.

Hike to the peak of Irazú Volcano to enjoy panoramic views.

 **Budget:**

Budget hostels start at $20 per night. Mid-range hotels cost $50 to $100 per night.

Meals: Local cafes serve wonderful meals for $5 to $10 per person. Upscale restaurants may charge extra.

Buses in the Central Valley are inexpensive (around $1 to $2 each ride). Taxi fares are also reasonable.

Entrance prices to attractions vary but are often reasonable.

 Getting there:

San José's Juan Santamaría International Airport (SJO) serves as the principal gateway.

From the airport, take a cab or shuttle to your hotel.

If you're already in Costa Rica, buses connect San José with other Central Valley cities.

Safety Tips: While Costa Rica is typically safe, be cautious in busy locations.

Due to the high altitude, use sunblock and remain hydrated.

Learn a few simple Spanish phrases; it will improve your experience!

Caribbean Coast: Laid-Back Vibes

Costa Rica's Caribbean coast entices visitors with its distinct combination of colors, culture, and laid-back atmosphere. Here's a more thorough look at this fascinating region:

Limon Province:
The Caribbean shore is well known as Limón province. It's a paradise where vivid jungles, beautiful beaches, and colorful towns coexist in perfect harmony.
Limón's Afro-Caribbean culture pervades everything—music, food, and architecture.

Culture and cuisine:
Local music: As you walk through the streets, you'll hear a harmonious blend of reggae, calypso, and salsa. Live music streams out of clubs and restaurants, creating a catchy beat.
Food: Get ready to experience a blend of Caribbean and Latin American tastes. Consider rice and beans, jerk chicken, coconut milk, tropical fruit, and fresh seafood. The village of Puerto Viejo is a gastronomic paradise.

Beach bliss: The Caribbean coast's beaches are paradise.

Playa Cocles is a long, broad beach immediately south of Puerto Viejo. Swim, surf, sunbathe, and visit beachfront bars and restaurants.

Punta Uva: About 4 miles south of Puerto Viejo, this gorgeous beach has calm seas ideal for swimming and snorkeling.

Playa Chiquita: This secluded beach, surrounded by palm trees and tropical jungle, is ideal for relaxing.

Playa Manzanillo is a remote and untouched beach located approximately 7 miles south of Puerto Viejo. Snorkel, swim, and explore the surrounding jungle.

Playa Negra: This black sand beach, located north of Puerto Viejo, is ideal for surfers.

Explore Gandoca-Manzanillo Wildlife Refuge and Cahuita National Park. Find howler monkeys, sloths, toucans, and sea turtles.

Do not miss the Jaguar Rescue Center in Puerto Viejo, where you may interact with rescued and healed animals.

Accommodation options vary from affordable hostels (about $20 per night) to mid-range hotels (50-100 per night).

Meals at neighborhood restaurants cost between $5 and $10 per person.

To get there, fly into Juan Santamaría International Airport (SJO) in San José.
From there, take a cab or shuttle to your Caribbean destination.

Tip: Use sunblock at higher altitudes.
Learn a few fundamental Spanish phrases; it will improve your experience.

Northern Plains: Nature's Playground.

Now, let's head to the Northern Plains, where nature reigns supreme. Here's a complete handbook.

Lush landscapes:
The Northern Plains have undulating hills, lush plains, and thick woods.
Arenal Volcano dominates the skyline, and its perfect cone shape is breathtaking.

Arenal Volcano National Park.
Hike through beautiful jungles, cross hanging bridges, and relax in natural hot springs.
Witness the occasional rumbling and lava pour from the towering Arenal.

Lake Arenal

This large reservoir provides watersports, fishing, and boat cruises.
Kayak along the tranquil waters, surrounded by lush hills.
La Fortuna, a lovely village near Arenal, is your doorway to adventure.
Zip line through the canopy, rappel down waterfalls, or go horseback riding.

Wildlife Encounters:

Keep a look out for howler monkeys, sloths, and colorful birds.
Take a guided night excursion to see nocturnal animals.
Hot springs and spa retreats:
Relax in natural thermal pools that provide views of Arenal.
Pamper yourself at exquisite spa resorts.

Budget and accommodations:

Accommodation in the Northern Plains caters to a variety of budgets:
Budget hostels start at $20 per night.
Mid-Range Hotels: Comfortable mid-range hotels cost $50 to $100 a night.
Luxury Resorts: For a special treat, try premium spa resorts with breathtaking views.

Getting there:

Fly into Juan Santamaría International Airport (SJO) in San José.

Following that, enjoy a picturesque drive or bus to the Northern Plains.

The trip is part of the adventure!

Tips for exploring the Northern Plains:

Layers are recommended because the weather might vary quickly owing to height. Bring both warm and light clothes.

If you plan on zip-lining or rappelling down a waterfall, dress comfortably and wear closed-toe shoes.

Local Cuisine: Try gallo pinto (rice and beans), a Costa Rican staple.

Arenal's Magic:

As the sun sets behind Arenal, the volcano comes alive with colorful lava flows—a breathtaking sight.

Guanacaste, Costa Rica

 Getting to Guanacaste

The Liberia Airport in Costa Rica is your gateway to Guanacaste. Look for direct flights from airports like LAX.

From Liberia, it's about a 30-45 minute drive to reach the popular resort area of the Papagayo Peninsula.
If you're not renting a car, pre-arrange transfers in advance.

What to Know Before Visiting Guanacaste

Language:
Spanish is the official language, but you'll find that English is widely spoken.
Currency & Money:
Most vendors accept USD and credit cards, but it's advisable to keep some local currency on hand.

Renting a Car:
Renting a car is a great way to explore the province. Book with Discover Cars for the best deals and coverage options.
Get full coverage insurance for peace of mind.

Best Time to Visit:
Guanacaste experiences a dry and wet season.
Plan your trip based on weather preferences:
Dry season (December to April) for sunny days.
Wet season (May to November) for lush green landscapes.

Things to Do in Guanacaste

Sunset Catamaran Tour:

Sail along the coast, enjoy breathtaking views, and maybe even spot dolphins or sea turtles.

Safari Boat Adventure in Palo Verde National Park:

Explore the mangroves, spot crocodiles, monkeys, and exotic birds.

Visit Tenorio Volcano National Park, Rio Celeste Waterfall, and Sloth Sanctuary:

Hike to the Rio Celeste Waterfall, known for its striking blue color.

Visit the Sloth Sanctuary and get up close to these adorable creatures.

Top Hotels in Guanacaste:

Andaz Costa Rica Resort at Peninsula Papagayo: Best overall hotel.

Four Seasons Resort Peninsula Papagayo: Best luxury hotel.

Secrets Papagayo: Best all-inclusive hotel.

El Mangroove, Autograph Collection: Best boutique hotel.

South Pacific Islands

How to Island Hop in the South Pacific?

Weather Considerations:
The islands experience dry and wet seasons.
Plan your trip based on weather preferences.

Best Time to Visit:
Weather is crucial. The dry season is ideal for most islands.
Start in Vanuatu (end of dry season) and finish in French Polynesia (wet season).

Island Hopping Tips:
No two islands are the same. Explore beyond the beaches.
Traveling to the far reaches requires careful planning and good timing.

Island-Hopping Essentials:
Vanuatu, Samoa, American Samoa, Cook Islands, Pitcairn Island, Easter Island, and French Polynesia await your discovery.

MUST-SEE ATTRACTIONS: YOUR BUCKET LIST

Arenal Volcano: Nature's Fireworks

 Getting There

La Fortuna, a charming town, serves as the gateway to Arenal Volcano.

If you're already in Costa Rica, you can start your adventure from various destinations, including:

- ✔ San José
- ✔ Papagayo Gulf
- ✔ Guanacaste
- ✔ Jaco Beach
- ✔ Manuel Antonio Beach
- ✔ El Coco Beach
- ✔ Potrero Beach
- ✔ Samara Beach
- ✔ Sarapiqui

 What to Do

Explore La Fortuna:

Take time to wander the village, dine in local restaurants, and soak in the laid-back atmosphere.

Arenal Volcano Hike & Hot Springs:

Embark on a nature hike around Arenal Volcano.

Witness the impressive volcanic landscape and learn about its history.

Afterward, relax in the natural hot springs—a perfect way to unwind.

Where to Stay
Consider these top hotels in La Fortuna:
Andaz Costa Rica Resort at Peninsula Papagayo: Best overall hotel.
Four Seasons Resort Peninsula Papagayo: Best luxury hotel.
Secrets Papagayo: Best all-inclusive hotel.
El Mangroove, Autograph Collection: Best boutique hotel.

Monteverde Cloud Forest: A Misty Wonderland

About Monteverde Cloud Forest Reserve
The Monteverde Cloud Forest Reserve was founded in 1972, making it one of the oldest private reserves in Costa Rica.

A graduate student named George Powell initiated the creation of the reserve after witnessing the harm caused by hunters and squatters in the Monteverde area.

Initially, it wasn't very popular, with only 431 visitors in 1975, most of whom were biologists. However, during the 1980s, tourism began to boom, and today, around 250,000 visitors explore this unique ecosystem each year.

What Makes It Special?
Lush Greenery:
The name "Monteverde" translates to "green mountain", and it's easy to see why—the area is blanketed in a lush, verdant forest.

The reserve spans 26,000 acres of cloud forest, home to a rich diversity of flora and fauna.

Cloud Forest Definition:
A cloud forest is a tropical forest that is constantly shrouded in heavy mist or fog.

Inside the forest, it's so moist that it's often covered in clouds.

Unique Microclimates:
Monteverde Cloud Forest Reserve comprises six ecological zones, each with its own microclimate and ecosystem.

It's home to over 100 mammal species, 400 bird species, and over 2,500 species of plants.

Where Is Monteverde Cloud Forest?
Located in the Cordillera de Tilarán mountain range, it runs parallel to the Pacific coast of Costa Rica.

The reserve is about 4 hours from San José, the capital city of Costa Rica, making it a popular day trip or weekend getaway destination.

What to Do in Monteverde

Explore the Trails:

Once on the trails, you'll lose sight of everyone, immersed in the misty wonder of the forest.

Encounter exotic plants, elusive animals, and breathtaking vistas.

Wildlife Spotting:

Keep your eyes peeled for jaguars, ocelots, and pumas—some of the most exotic creatures on the planet.

Birdwatchers will be delighted by the diverse avian species.

Santa Elena Cloud Forest Reserve:

For a different cloud forest experience, visit the Reserva Santa Elena nearby.

Manuel Antonio National Park: Wildlife Meets Beaches

 Location and Access

Manuel Antonio National Park is located on Costa Rica's southwest coast, approximately 3.5 hours' drive from San Jose.

This stunning park is known for its incredible wildlife, the Manuel Antonio National Park, and, of course, its beautiful beaches.

Why Visit?
Breathtaking Beaches:
Manuel Antonio is home to some of the best beaches in all of Costa Rica.

The natural coasts and beaches rival those of world-class destinations.

Whether you're into nature, party scenes, or simply relaxing on iconic Central American beaches, Manuel Antonio has it all.

Wildlife Abounds:
The park's unique mix of habitats makes wildlife viewing easy.

Within its boundaries, you'll find primary and secondary rainforests, mangroves, wetlands, and beaches.

Over 346 plant species, 350 bird species, and 100 mammal species call this area home.

Beaches Inside the Park
Playa Manuel Antonio:
A crescent-shaped gem within the national park.

Wildlife is abundant, and the beach offers a unique mix of relaxation and adventure.

Playa Espadilla Sur:

Separated from Playa Manuel Antonio by a natural land bridge.

Gorgeous white sand and clear waters.

Playa Gemelas:

Another beautiful beach within the park.

Perfect for swimming and snorkeling.

Beaches Outside the Park

Playa Espadilla Norte:

Just outside the park boundaries.

Offers a different vibe and more space.

Playa Biesanz:

Secluded and tranquil.

Ideal for escaping the crowds.

Palo Seco Beach:

Located nearby.

A peaceful spot to unwind.

Tortuguero National Park: A Turtle Haven

 **Location and Access**

Tortuguero National Park is situated on the northeastern Caribbean coast of Costa Rica.

Although it's a remote paradise, accessible only by airplane or boat, it ranks as the third-most visited park in the country.

Why Visit?
Sea Turtle Nesting:
Tortuguero is renowned for its sea turtle nesting season, which typically occurs from July to October.
Hundreds of sea turtles arrive on the park's beaches to lay their eggs.
Witness this incredible spectacle by joining guided night tours.

Biodiversity:
Beyond sea turtles, Tortuguero is a haven for biodiversity.
Encounter howler monkeys, capuchin monkeys, jaguars, ocelots, river otters, manatees, and countless bird species.
The park's complex system of rivers, lagoons, and wetlands provides a rich habitat for these creatures.

Canal Tours:
Explore the park's extensive network of canals and rivers by taking a guided boat tour.
Spot monkeys, sloths, caimans, basilisk lizards, and various bird species like toucans and herons.

Lush Rainforest:
Tortuguero is part of the larger Tortuguero Conservation Area, which includes the national park and protected areas.
Immerse yourself in lush tropical rainforests and swamps—a unique and immersive natural experience.
Beaches of Tortuguero
While the beaches of Tortuguero are not typical for swimming or sunbathing, they are wildly beautiful.
The coastline provides sea turtles a protected place to lay their eggs.
Explore the rugged black sand beaches and witness the untamed beauty.

Corcovado National Park: Biodiversity Galore

Location and Access
Corcovado National Park graces the Osa Peninsula in southwest Costa Rica.
This remote paradise, accessible only by guided tours, is a sanctuary for nature enthusiasts.

Why Visit?
Incredible Biodiversity:

Corcovado boasts 2.5% of the world's biodiversity—an astounding statistic.

Here, you'll encounter an astonishing variety of plant and animal life.

Rare and Endangered Species:

Baird's tapir, the largest land mammal in Central America, calls Corcovado home.

Spot the majestic Harpy eagle, one of the world's most powerful eagles.

Other inhabitants include ocelots, Bull sharks, pumas, and White-faced capuchin monkeys.

Coastal Beauty

Corcovado's 46 kilometers of sandy beaches meet the Pacific Ocean.

Explore the rugged coastline, where sea turtles nest and mangrove forests thrive.

Wildlife Encounters

Monkeys: You'll see lots of monkeys—squirrel monkeys, mantled howlers, and more.

Big Cats: Elusive jaguars, pumas, ocelots, and margays roam the rainforest.

Birdwatching: Scarlet macaws, hummingbirds, and 220 butterfly species fill the skies.

Beaches of Corcovado

While not typical for swimming, the 23 miles of beaches are wildly beautiful.

Witness sea turtles nesting along these pristine shores.

BEACH BLISS: COASTAL ESCAPES

Pacific Gems: Playa Tamarindo, Playa Santa Teresa

Costa Rica's coastlines are a paradise for beach lovers, offering a diverse array of sandy retreats from the bustling Pacific shores to the tranquil Caribbean waters. Each beach has its unique charm, making the country a perfect destination for those seeking sun, surf, and sand.

Playa Tamarindo:

Nestled in the province of Guanacaste, Playa Tamarindo is one of Costa Rica's most popular and accessible beaches. Known for its excellent surf conditions, vibrant nightlife, and stunning sunsets, Tamarindo is a hub of activity, attracting surfers, families, and nature enthusiasts alike.

Activities: Surfing is the main draw, with schools and rentals available for all levels. Other activities include snorkeling, stand-up paddleboarding, and sport fishing. The beach is also a nesting ground for leatherback turtles, offering unique wildlife watching opportunities.
Amenities: Tamarindo boasts a wide range of accommodations, from luxury resorts to budget hostels. The town is filled with restaurants, bars, and

shops, providing plenty of options for dining and entertainment.

Getting There: Tamarindo is easily accessible by car or shuttle from Liberia International Airport, about an hour's drive away.

Playa Santa Teresa

Located on the Nicoya Peninsula, Playa Santa Teresa is a laid-back beach town known for its surf, yoga, and bohemian vibe. The beach stretches for miles, offering pristine sands and crystal-clear waters, making it an ideal spot for relaxation and outdoor activities.

Activities: Surfing is the main attraction, with consistent waves suitable for all levels. Yoga retreats and wellness centers are abundant, offering a peaceful escape. Horseback riding, hiking, and ATV tours are also popular ways to explore the surrounding natural beauty.

Amenities: Santa Teresa offers a variety of accommodations, from luxury villas to cozy guesthouses. The town has a vibrant food scene, with beachfront cafes, international restaurants, and local sodas (small eateries) serving delicious Costa Rican cuisine.

Getting There: The most common route is to take a ferry from Puntarenas to Paquera and then drive to

Santa Teresa. Alternatively, there are domestic flights to nearby Tambor Airport, followed by a short drive.

Caribbean Retreats: Puerto Viejo, Cahuita

Costa Rica's Caribbean coast is a treasure trove of lush landscapes, vibrant cultures, and tranquil beaches. Two standout destinations in this region are Puerto Viejo and Cahuita, each offering a unique blend of natural beauty and laid-back charm.

Puerto Viejo:

Situated in the province of Limón, Puerto Viejo is a lively beach town known for its Afro-Caribbean influence, eclectic vibe, and stunning beaches. The town is a melting pot of cultures, reflected in its music, cuisine, and festivals.

Attractions: Puerto Viejo is famous for its surf break at Salsa Brava, attracting surfers from around the world. The town is surrounded by beautiful beaches like Playa Cocles and Playa Chiquita, perfect for swimming and sunbathing. The nearby Jaguar Rescue Center offers a chance to see and learn about local wildlife.

Culture and Cuisine: The town's vibrant nightlife includes reggae bars, live music, and dance clubs. Culinary delights range from traditional Caribbean dishes like rice and beans with coconut to international cuisine.

Getting There: Puerto Viejo is about a four-hour drive from San José, with regular bus services and shuttle options available.

Cahuita:

A short drive north of Puerto Viejo lies Cahuita, a serene village that's home to the stunning Cahuita National Park. This area is known for its relaxed atmosphere, beautiful beaches, and rich biodiversity.

Attractions: Cahuita National Park is a highlight, offering hiking trails, white sandy beaches, and excellent snorkeling opportunities in its coral reefs. The park is home to a variety of wildlife, including monkeys, sloths, and tropical birds.

Culture and Cuisine: Cahuita has a laid-back vibe, with a slower pace of life than Puerto Viejo. The village has a selection of cozy restaurants and bars serving local and international dishes, with an emphasis on fresh seafood.

Getting There: Cahuita is easily accessible from Puerto Viejo by bus or car, and it's about a 3.5-hour drive from San José.

Beach Activities: Surfing, Snorkeling, Relaxing

The beaches of Costa Rica's Caribbean coast offer a plethora of activities to suit every traveler's preferences:

Surfing: Puerto Viejo's Salsa Brava is renowned for its powerful waves, attracting experienced surfers. For beginners, there are gentler spots along the coast where surf schools offer lessons and equipment rentals.

Snorkeling: The clear waters and coral reefs of Cahuita National Park provide excellent snorkeling opportunities. You can explore the vibrant underwater world, teeming with colorful fish, sea turtles, and other marine life.

Relaxing: Sometimes, the best beach activity is simply to relax and soak up the sun. Both Puerto Viejo and Cahuita boast pristine beaches where you can unwind in a hammock, take leisurely strolls along the shore, or enjoy a refreshing swim in the warm Caribbean Sea.

Coastal Conservation: Respecting Marine Life

Costa Rica's dedication to environmental protection includes its coastal and marine environments, which are critical for biodiversity, tourism, and local livelihoods. Respecting marine life is not just an ethical duty, but also necessary for the survival of these natural wonders.

Here are some important issues of coastal conservation in Costa Rica.

Protected areas:

Many of Costa Rica's coastal sections have been declared as protected areas, including national parks, animal refuges, and marine reserves. These zones are intended to preserve ecosystems, protect endangered species, and maintain ecological equilibrium.

Notable examples are the Marino Ballena National Park, which is famous for its whale watching possibilities, and the Cocos Island National Park, a UNESCO World Heritage Site noted for its diverse marine life and diving options.

Sustainable tourism:

Ecotourism is a key component of Costa Rica's conservation strategy. Tour operators and local communities are urged to use sustainable methods such as reducing environmental damage, promoting responsible wildlife watching, and contributing to conservation initiatives.

Visitors are encouraged to follow standards when participating in activities such as snorkeling, diving, and animal viewing to minimize disruption to marine ecosystems.

Community involvement:
Local communities play an important role in coastal protection. Initiatives like community-managed reserves, sustainable fishing techniques, and environmental education initiatives assist communities conserve their natural resources.

By incorporating communities in conservation activities, Costa Rica promotes stewardship and shared responsibility for the health of its coastal and marine resources.

Research and monitoring:
Ongoing scientific study and monitoring are critical for better understanding marine ecosystems and solving conservation issues. Costa Rica works with international organizations, universities, and research institutions to study marine biodiversity, monitor coral reefs, and track migratory species.

This study informs conservation policy, identifies dangers, and directs management efforts to safeguard marine species.

Threats and challenges:
Despite these efforts, Costa Rica's coastal and marine ecosystems are under threat from pollution, overfishing, climate change, and habitat degradation. To address these difficulties, a multifaceted approach is required, which includes stronger enforcement of environmental laws, international cooperation, and continuing conservation funding.

Temple of Music

URBAN ADVENTURES: CITY LIFE IN COSTA RICA

Costa Rica is not only a haven for nature lovers but also a vibrant urban destination with lively cities full of culture, history, and entertainment. Among these, the capital city, San José, stands out as the cultural heartbeat of the country.

San José: Cultural Heartbeat

Overview:

San José, nestled in the Central Valley, is the bustling capital of Costa Rica. It's a city where traditional and modern elements blend seamlessly, offering visitors a rich cultural experience. From historical landmarks and museums to contemporary art galleries and theaters, San José is a hub of Costa Rican culture and creativity.

Key Attractions:

National Theatre of Costa Rica (Teatro Nacional): An architectural masterpiece and a symbol of the country's cultural heritage. It hosts a variety of performances, including opera, ballet, and classical music.

Central Market (Mercado Central): A lively market where you can experience the local way of life, taste traditional foods, and shop for souvenirs and crafts.

Museum of Costa Rican Art (Museo de Arte Costarricense): Located in La Sabana Park, this museum showcases a collection of national art, from pre-Columbian pieces to contemporary works.
Gold Museum (Museo del Oro Precolombino): A fascinating museum displaying an extensive collection of pre-Columbian gold artifacts, providing insight into the country's ancient cultures.
Jade Museum (Museo del Jade): Home to the world's largest collection of American jade, featuring exquisite pieces that highlight the craftsmanship of the indigenous peoples.

Cultural Experiences:

Walking Tours: Explore the city's vibrant neighborhoods, historical buildings, and hidden gems on a guided walking tour.
Culinary Scene: San José offers a diverse culinary landscape, from traditional Costa Rican cuisine to international flavors. Don't miss the chance to try dishes like gallo pinto, casado, and ceviche.
Art Galleries and Exhibitions: The city is dotted with art galleries showcasing the works of local and international artists. Explore the contemporary art scene and attend exhibitions to immerse yourself in the creative spirit of San José.

Festivals and Events: Throughout the year, San José hosts various cultural events, including music festivals, dance performances, and art fairs. Check the local event calendar to experience the city's vibrant cultural life.

▣ Practical tips:

Getting Around: San José has an extensive public transportation system, including buses and taxis. For a more immersive experience, consider exploring the city on foot or renting a bicycle.

Safety: Like any urban center, it's important to stay vigilant and aware of your surroundings. Keep your valuables secure and be cautious in crowded areas.

Accommodations: The city offers a wide range of accommodations, from luxury hotels to budget-friendly hostels, catering to all preferences and budgets.

Limón: Caribbean Flavor

Limón, located on Costa Rica's Caribbean coast, is a dynamic port city with rich Afro-Caribbean culture, beautiful woods, and magnificent beaches. It serves as a gateway to the country's natural beauty and distinct cultural experiences on the Caribbean side.

Key Attractions:

Veragua Rainforest Park: A must-see for nature enthusiasts, this park has canopy tours, a reptile display, and a butterfly garden that showcase the region's rich flora and wildlife.

Tortuguero National Park: This secluded park, accessible only by boat or plane, is known for its canals, tropical rainforest, and sea turtle nesting sites.

Cahuita National Park, located near Cahuita, is well-known for its coral reefs, white sandy beaches, and hiking paths through the coastal jungle.

Afro-Caribbean Culture: Limón is the core of Costa Rica's Afro-Caribbean community. Experience the vivid music, dancing, and food, which includes coconut milk-cooked rice and beans and spicy jerk chicken.

Cultural Experiences:

Carnival: Limón's annual carnival, celebrated in October, is a vibrant event including parades, music, dancing, and colorful costumes that highlight the city's Afro-Caribbean roots.

Reggae, calypso, and soca music are essential components of Limón's cultural identity. Don't pass up the opportunity to enjoy live music performances and dance to the rhythmic beats.

Culinary Delights: Limón's cuisine stands apart from the rest of Costa Rica, having a strong Caribbean flavor. Try traditional foods such as patí (spicy pork pastry), rondón (coconut milk-based seafood stew), and plantintá (sweet plantain pie).

⊞ **Practical tips:**

Getting Around: Limón is a tiny city with several attractions within walking reach. Buses and taxis are easily accessible to explore the nearby districts.

Safety: As in any city, you should remain alert and aware of your surroundings, especially after dark. Stick to well-lit, popular locations.

Limón has a variety of lodgings to suit all interests and budgets, ranging from beachside hotels to small guesthouses.

Alajuela: Volcanoes and History

Overview:

Alajuela, located in the central part of Costa Rica, is a region steeped in history and natural beauty. It is home to the country's most active volcano, Arenal, and is a gateway to a variety of outdoor adventures and historical sites.

Key Attractions:

Arenal Volcano: Dominating the landscape, Arenal is a must-see for its perfect conical shape and frequent eruptions. The surrounding Arenal Volcano National Park offers hiking trails, hot springs, and opportunities for wildlife watching.

La Fortuna Waterfall: A short drive from the Arenal Volcano, this stunning waterfall plunges 70 meters into a crystal-clear pool, perfect for a refreshing swim.

Poás Volcano National Park: Home to one of the world's largest accessible volcanic craters, Poás offers breathtaking views and a unique lunar landscape.

Historic Sites: Alajuela is rich in history, with landmarks such as the Juan Santamaría Museum, dedicated to Costa Rica's national hero, and the colonial churches in the town of Grecia.

Cultural Experiences:

Local Festivals: Alajuela hosts various festivals throughout the year, celebrating everything from traditional music and dance to local agriculture.

Cuisine: The region's fertile lands produce a bounty of fruits and vegetables. Be sure to try local dishes like olla de carne (a hearty beef stew) and tamales.

⊞ **Practical tips:**

Getting Around: Alajuela is well-connected by roads and public transportation, making it easy to explore the region's attractions.

Accommodations: The area offers a range of accommodations, from luxury resorts near the Arenal Volcano to cozy bed and breakfasts in the historic town center.

Heredia: Coffee and Flowers

Overview:

Heredia, often referred to as the "City of Flowers," is located in the central highlands of Costa Rica. It is known for its lush landscapes, coffee plantations, and charming colonial architecture.

⊞ **Key Attractions:**

Coffee Tours: Heredia is at the heart of Costa Rica's coffee region. Visitors can tour coffee plantations to learn about the production process and sample some of the world's finest coffee.

Barva Volcano: Part of Braulio Carrillo National Park, Barva Volcano offers hiking trails through cloud forests and opportunities to spot a variety of bird species.

Historic Heredia: The city center boasts well-preserved colonial buildings, including the Heredia Cathedral and El Fortín, a historic tower that is a symbol of the city.

🎎Cultural Experiences:

Flower Festivals: As the City of Flowers, Heredia hosts vibrant festivals celebrating its floral heritage, with colorful parades and floral displays.

Arts and Crafts: The region is known for its artisanal products, including handcrafted pottery and traditional Costa Rican souvenirs.

🔢 Practical tips:

Getting Around: Heredia is easily navigable on foot, especially the historic city center. For exploring the surrounding areas, buses and taxis are available.

Accommodations: Heredia offers a variety of accommodations, from historic hotels in the city center to countryside lodges surrounded by coffee plantations.

Cartago: Ancient Capital

Overview:

Cartago, located in Costa Rica's central highlands, is a historically and culturally significant city. As Costa Rica's first capital, it was an important cultural and religious center throughout the colonial period and continues to be so today. Cartago, with its historical landmarks, attractive natural settings, and religious importance, provides a unique perspective on Costa Rica's legacy.

Key Attractions:

The Basilica of Our Lady of the Angels (Basílica de Nuestra Señora de los Ángeles) is a popular pilgrimage destination, attracting thousands of pilgrims annually, particularly on August 2nd to celebrate Costa Rica's patron saint, La Negrita.

At Irazú Volcano National Park, tourists may enjoy spectacular views of both the Pacific and Atlantic Oceans from the peak. The park's lunar-like scenery and bright crater lakes are must-sees.

The remains of Ujarrás, one of Costa Rica's oldest churches, are a testimony to the country's colonial past. The surrounding gardens and views of the Orosi Valley create a tranquil and scenic setting.

Lankester Botanical Garden: This globally famous garden houses a large collection of orchids, bromeliads, and other tropical plants, highlighting the region's diverse ecosystem.

Cultural Experiences:

Cartago is renowned for its magnificent Semana Santa (Holy Week) processions, which are among the most traditional and solemn in the country.

nearby Cuisine: Try traditional Cartago meals such as tamal asado (a sweet corn cake) and fish from the nearby mountain streams.

Artisanal crafts: The area is well-known for its ceramics and woodworking. Visit local markets and workshops to observe craftspeople in action and buy one-of-a-kind mementos.

Practical tips:

Getting Around: Cartago is well served by public transit, including buses and the urban rail from San José. The city is also bike-friendly, with designated lanes and bike rental options.

Accommodations: Cartago has a variety of options, including historic hotels in the city center and lovely cottages in the surrounding countryside.

Weather: Because of its high altitude, the city has a colder climate than other sections of Costa Rica, so dress warmly in the evenings.

Culinary Journey: Tasting Costa Rica

Traditional Dishes: Gallo Pinto, Casado, Ceviche

Costa Rican cuisine is a delectable fusion of Spanish, Indigenous, and African influences, resulting in a wide range of flavors and textures that will satisfy any palette. Here are some classic foods that you should taste on your culinary tour in Costa Rica:

**Gallo Pinto:**

Gallo Pinto, or "spotted rooster," is Costa Rica's national dish. It's a robust and tasty rice and black bean dish that is frequently seasoned with onions, bell peppers, cilantro, and a unique sauce known as Salsa Lizano.

When To Eat: Gallo Pinto, which is typically eaten for breakfast, is an excellent way to start the day with a boost of energy. It can also be served as a side dish with lunch or dinner.

Pairing: It's often served with eggs, plantains, avocado, and tortillas for a complete and fulfilling dinner.

Casado:

Casado is a classic Costa Rican lunch dish that features the country's core foods. Rice, beans, salad, plantains, and a protein of choice (chicken, beef, fish, or hog) are common ingredients.

When to Eat: Casado is a popular lunch choice, delivering a well-balanced and satisfying meal to fuel your afternoon activities.

Variations: The components of a Casado can alter according on the locale and the cook, making it a dish that can be enjoyed numerous times with diverse flavors.

Ceviche:

Ceviche is a pleasant and zesty seafood meal made with fresh fish or shrimp marinated in lime juice and combined with onions, cilantro, and bell peppers.

Ceviche is frequently served as an appetizer or light meal, making it ideal for a hot day or as a precursor to a bigger feast.

Serving Tip: Tortilla chips or soda crackers are frequently given to balance out the dish's acidity.

Other must-try dishes:

Tamales are a classic holiday dish fashioned from maize dough and filled with a variety of ingredients such as pork, rice, and vegetables before being wrapped in banana leaves and cooked.

Arroz with Pollo: A savory chicken and rice meal seasoned with herbs and spices, typically eaten with a salad or vegetables.

Sopa Negra: A hearty black bean soup served with cooked eggs, rice, and tortillas.

Culinary tips:

Enjoy the Flavors: Costa Rican food is primarily on fresh, basic ingredients. Take time to absorb the flavors and appreciate the dishes' simplicity.

Street cuisine is a must-try for an authentic experience of local life. You'll discover tasty alternatives like as empanadas, churros, and fresh fruit.

Local Markets: Visit local markets to try a range of fruits and vegetables native to the region, such as pejibaye, guanabana, and mamón chino.

Street Food: Where to Find the Best Bites

Costa Rica's street food scene is a dynamic and delectable component of the country's culinary tradition. Here are some of the finest bites:

San José:

Central Market (Mercado Central): This lively market in the center of the city offers a wide range of street food options, from traditional appetizers like empanadas and chorreadas (corn pancakes) to sweet delicacies like tres leches cake.

On weekends, vendors set up throughout this vast park, selling anything from fresh coconut water to chicharrones (fried hog bellies).

Barrio Escalante: This fashionable area is recognized for its culinary culture, which includes street food booths and food trucks that provide gourmet snacks and fusion meals.

Limon:

Puerto Viejo: This laid-back seaside town is an excellent place to sample Caribbean-inspired street cuisine like patties (spicy meat pastry) and rondón (a coconut milk stew).

Cahuita: The streets around Cahuita National Park are lined with merchants offering fresh seafood, such as ceviche and grilled fish.

Guanacaste:

Tamarindo: This renowned surfing town has a thriving street food scene, with vendors offering anything from smoothie bowls to BBQ skewers.

Liberia's central market is a great spot to taste traditional Guanacaste foods like rosquillas (cornmeal biscuits) and tanelas (sweet corn fritters).

Puntarenas:

Monteverde's night market serves a range of street foods, including local cheese, handmade bread, and homemade jams.

Puntarenas City's beachside promenade is dotted with shops serving local delicacies like as vigorón (a cabbage and yucca dish) and copos (shaved ice with condensed milk).

Tips to Enjoy Street Food:

Look for Busy Stands: A large queue typically indicates that the food is fresh and tasty.

Try Something New: Don't be scared to venture outside of your comfort zone and try new cuisine.

Ask for Recommendations: Locals are frequently eager to offer their favorite sites and must-try dishes.

Practice food safety. Select vendors with clean booths and fresh ingredients. If you have a sensitive stomach, avoid raw meals and unpeeled fruits.

Dining Etiquette: Local Customs

Understanding local eating etiquette is an essential component of understanding Costa Rican culture. Here are some customs to consider when dining in Costa Rica:

Greeting and Seating:
It is usual to welcome everyone at the table with a handshake or a nod as you arrive.

Wait to be seated by the host or server, particularly in formal situations or at a person's house.

Table manners:
Once you're seated, place your napkin on your lap. It's an example of excellent manners.

Most meals require utensils, including those that are called finger foods in other cultures. It is okay to eat tortillas and bread with your fingers.

Keep your elbows off the table and your hands visible when eating.

It is courteous to taste a little of everything provided to you, especially while dining at someone's house.

Eating Pace:
Costa Ricans eat at a casual pace. Take your time and enjoy the food and conversation.

It is considered disrespectful to speed through your dinner or begin eating before the host or the oldest member at the table.

Conversation:

Keep the discussion lighthearted and welcoming. Avoid contentious issues like politics and religion.

It's customary to discuss family, travel, and cuisine.

Asking for Seconds:

Asking for seconds is a compliment to the cook, particularly in a home environment. Wait until everyone has been served before asking.

Finishing the Meal:

Place your knife and fork on your plate, handles facing right, to indicate that you are finished.

Compliment the cook or host on their dinner. A simple "¡Qué rico!" (How excellent!) would be appreciated.

Tipping:

In restaurants, a 10% service fee is frequently included on the bill. It is usual to leave an extra little tip (about 5%) if the service was extraordinary.

Tipping for other services, such as taxis or tour guides, is optional but appreciated for good service.

Vegetarian and Vegan Options: Finding Green Eats

Costa Rica's abundance of fresh fruit and developing health-conscious society make it an appealing destination for vegetarians and vegans.

Here's how to locate green foods around the country:

 **Traditional dishes:**

Gallo Pinto: This traditional Costa Rican breakfast of rice and beans is often vegan. Just make sure to inquire if it is prepared without animal fats.

Casado: A classic meal of rice, beans, salad, and plantains. Ask for it "sin carne" (without meat), and make sure the beans are not cooked with animal components.

Arroz with Vegetales: Rice with vegetables is a regular meal served at most local restaurants.

Vegetarian Empanadas: Many restaurants provide empanadas loaded with veggies or cheese.

Vegetarian and vegan restaurants:

San José: The capital city is home to an increasing number of vegetarian and vegan eateries that provide anything from local delicacies to foreign cuisine. Look for restaurants such as "Mantras Veggie Café" and "Luv Burger."

Popular tourist locations like as La Fortuna, Monteverde, and Tamarindo provide a variety of vegetarian and vegan food alternatives.

Many communities offer health food stores where vegetarians and vegans may buy meat replacements, dairy-free foods, and organic fruit.

Tips for eating out:

Communicate: Not all establishments are familiar with vegans, so be precise about your dietary needs. Phrases like "soy vegetariano/a" (I am vegetarian) and "soy vegano/a" (I am vegan) are useful.

Customize: Don't be afraid to request menu alterations, such as changing meat with avocado or adding more veggies.

Search for "Soda" eateries: These neighborhood eateries frequently provide home-style meals and may readily accommodate vegetarian demands.

Farmers' Markets:

Local farmers' markets, or "ferias," are an excellent place to find fresh fruits, vegetables, legumes, and grains. It's also an opportunity to support local farmers while discovering new delicacies.

Vegetarian Friendly Accommodations:
Some eco-lodges and wellness resorts in Costa Rica include vegetarian or vegan food alternatives for health-conscious guests.

AFTER DARK: COSTA RICA'S NIGHTLIFE

Hotspots for Partying: Best Bars and Clubs

Costa Rica's nightlife is as active and diversified as its natural surroundings, with a wide range of venues for partying, dancing, and mingling. Here are some of the top pubs and clubs for experiencing Costa Rica's vibrant after-dark scene:

San José:

Castro's Bar and Disco is a renowned dance place that plays a combination of Latin and worldwide music. It's famous for its vibrant atmosphere and themed nights.

El Pueblo: This complex is home to a number of pubs and clubs, each with their own distinct ambiance. Everyone may find something they enjoy, from salsa dancing at La Pachanga to electronic sounds at Club Vertigo.

Rapsodia Lounge & Nightclub: A sophisticated and modern club with a fashionable audience, noted for its elegant design and top-tier DJs.

Jacó:

Le Loft: A favorite of both residents and visitors, this club is recognized for its lively atmosphere and superb music, which ranges from reggae to electronica.

Orange Pub: A bustling establishment that frequently presents live music and DJs, attracting a younger population eager to dance and have a good time.

Tamarindo:

Crazy Monkey Bar: Located in the Tamarindo Vista Villas, this bar is well-known for its Friday night events, which feature breathtaking ocean views and a vibrant dance floor.

Pacifico Bar: A renowned outdoor bar noted for its relaxed atmosphere, live music, and delicious drinks. It's a terrific spot to mix with locals and other travellers.

Puerto Viejo:

Lazy Monday at Stanford's: This beachfront pub offers live reggae music, fire performances, and a relaxing Caribbean vibe.

Salsa Brava: Named after the famed surf break, this club is a popular dance destination that plays a mix of Latin and international music.

Tips for Enjoying Nightlife in Costa Rica:

Dress Code: While coastal communities are more casual, clubs in cities like San José may have a dress code, so make sure to check ahead of time.

Consider using a cab or using ride-sharing service for safe transit to and from entertainment locations, particularly late at night.

Safety: Keep an eye on your possessions and stay aware of your surroundings. It's usually better to go out in groups.
The legal drinking age in Costa Rica is 18. Be prepared to present identification in pubs and clubs.

Cultural Nights: Live Music and Dance

Costa Rica's rich cultural tapestry is vividly showcased through its live music and dance scenes, offering visitors a chance to immerse themselves in the country's artistic traditions. Here's where you can experience the best of Costa Rican cultural nights:

San José
Jazz Café: With locations in San Pedro and Escazú, Jazz Café is a renowned venue for live music, featuring everything from jazz and blues to Latin and rock.
Teatro Nacional: This historic theater hosts a variety of cultural performances, including classical music concerts, ballet, and traditional folkloric dance shows.
El Cuartel de la Boca del Monte: A popular spot among locals, this bar and music venue showcases live bands playing a range of genres, from salsa to indie rock.

Guanacaste

Guanacaste Nights: This annual event celebrates the region's folkloric music and dance, featuring performances by local artists and groups.

Tamarindo Night Market: Held every Thursday evening, this market features live music, dance performances, and local artisans selling their crafts.

Puerto Viejo

Caribeans Chocolate & Coffee: Enjoy live reggae and calypso music at this café and chocolate factory, which hosts regular music nights.

Hot Rocks: This lively bar and restaurant often features live bands and DJs, with a dance floor that heats up as the night goes on.

Monteverde

Monteverde Music Festival: This annual festival brings together national and international musicians for a series of concerts set against the backdrop of the cloud forest.

Tips for Enjoying Cultural Nights

Check Local Listings: For the most up-to-date information on live music and dance events, check local listings or ask at your accommodation.

Arrive Early: Popular venues can fill up quickly, especially on weekends, so it's a good idea to arrive early to secure a good spot.

Dress Appropriately: While Costa Rica is generally casual, some cultural events or venues may have a more formal dress code.

Embrace the Experience: Don't be shy to join in on the dancing, especially if it's a style you're not familiar with. Locals are often happy to share their dance moves with visitors.

Local Festivals: Joining the Celebration

Costa Rica is a country that enjoys celebrating, with several local festivals throughout the year that highlight its rich culture, customs, and natural beauty. Here are some of the most popular and exciting events you may participate in.

Fiesta de los Diablitos
Location: Boruca and Rey Curré Indigenous Reserves
Date: Late December/early January
Description: The "Festival of the Little Devils" is a traditional indigenous event that represents the Boruca people's resistance against Spanish colonization. It includes extravagant masks, costumes, music, and dancing.

Palmares Festival
Location: Palmares
Date: mid-January.
The Palmares Festival is one of the country's largest and most anticipated events, with music, bullfights (without killing the bull), street markets, and a horse procession known as a "tope."

Envision Festival
Location: Uvita.
Date: Late February/early March
Envision is a festival that blends music, art, yoga, and sustainability, attracting a worldwide audience wanting to celebrate in nature.

Semana Santa (holy week)
Location: Nationwide.
Date: The week before to Easter Sunday
Semana Santa is a major religious event in Costa Rica, with processions, reenactments of the Passion of Christ, and special masses held in places such as San José and Cartago.

The International Festival of Arts (FIA)
Location: San José.
Date: Typically in April.

This foreign Arts Festival celebrates music, dance, theater, and visual arts, showcasing both local and foreign performers.

Carnival and Limón Provincial Day:
Location: Limón.
Date: October 12th and surrounding days
Limón's carnival is a colorful celebration of Afro-Caribbean culture, with parades, music, dancing, and traditional dishes, and it coincides with Columbus Day in Costa Rica.

The Festival of Lights (Festival de la Luz)
Location: San José.
Date: mid-December.
Description: This celebration kicks off the Christmas season with a nighttime procession of floats, dancers, and marching bands decorated with beautiful lights.

Tips to Enjoy Local Festivals:
Plan Ahead: Accommodations and transportation often fill up fast during big events, so book early.
Stay hydrated: Costa Rica may get hot, especially during outdoor celebrations. Drink plenty of water and apply sunscreen.
Embrace Local Traditions: Festivals provide an excellent opportunity to immerse oneself in Costa

Rican culture. Try local delicacies, participate in events, and interact with the people.

Be Respectful: Keep in mind that some events, particularly those with religious or indigenous significance, have a significant impact on the local community. Show respect for traditions and customs.

Outdoor Thrills: Adventures in Nature

Costa Rica is a sanctuary for outdoor enthusiasts, with a diverse choice of activities situated in magnificent natural scenery. From lush rainforests to stunning volcanoes, the country's various ecosystems provide an ideal setting for adventure.

Hiking Trails: Explore the Great Outdoors

Arenal Volcano National Park.
Trail: Arenal Volcano Hike Description: This path provides amazing views of the Arenal Volcano and surrounding jungle. Hikers can witness lava flows from previous eruptions and may encounter fauna such as monkeys, toucans, and coatis.
Difficulty: Moderate Monteverde Cloud Forest Reserve

Trail: Sendero Bosque Nuboso
Description: This walk leads you through the heart of the cloud forest, where you can see the unique ecology with its hanging moss, ferns, and various birds, including the stunning quetzal.
Difficulty: Easy to Moderate
Corcovado National Park.

Trail: La Leona to Sirena Station.
This strenuous journey takes you through one of the world's most biodiverse areas, with chances to view tapirs, scarlet macaws, and even jaguars.
Difficulty: Challenging: Rincón de la Vieja National Park.

Trail: Las Pailas Loop.
This path provides a unique experience due to its volcanic activity, which includes bubbling mud pots, fumaroles, and hot springs. It's also an excellent site to see wildlife such as iguanas and howler monkeys.
The difficulty is moderate.
Manuel Antonio National Park:

Trail: The Punta Catedral Trail
Description: This gorgeous walk winds around the park's peninsula, providing breathtaking ocean vistas, magnificent beaches, and the opportunity to watch sloths and capuchin monkeys.
Difficulty: Easy to Moderate

Tips For Hiking in Costa Rica:
Start Early: To minimize the heat and improve your chances of viewing animals, begin your treks early in the morning.
Stay Hydrated: Bring lots of water, especially for longer walks, since the weather may be hot and humid.
Wear Appropriate Gear: Good hiking shoes, light clothes, and bug repellent are required.
Respect nature by staying on defined routes, not feeding wildlife, and taking all rubbish with you to maintain the natural beauty of these locations.

Surf's Up: Catching Waves

Costa Rica is a surfer's paradise, with some of the world's greatest waves on its Pacific and Caribbean coasts. Whether you're a seasoned veteran or a newbie looking for your first wave, there's a place for you. Here are some of the best surf spots in Costa Rica:

Tamarindo (Guanacaste)
Level: Beginning to Intermediate
Tamarindo is a famous surfing destination with a range of breakers appropriate for all skill levels. The major beach break has dependable waves, but adjacent Playa Langosta and Playa Grande provide more difficult possibilities.

Santa Teresa (the Nicoya Peninsula)
Level: Intermediate to Advanced
Santa Teresa is famous for its constant surf and stunning beaches. The region has a combination of beach and point breaks, with waves that may be extremely strong.

Nosara (the Nicoya Peninsula)
Level: Beginning to Intermediate
Nosara's Playa Guiones is ideal for novices, with calm waves and extensive sandy beaches. There are

numerous surf schools in the vicinity that provide training and board rentals.

Jaco, Central Pacific Coast

Level: Beginner to Advanced

Jaco is a lively surf town with a beach break appropriate for all skill levels. Nearby Playa Hermosa is well-known for its big waves and is a popular location for surf competitions.

Pavones (South Pacific Coast)

Level: Advanced Description: Pavones has one of the world's longest left-hand point breaks. The waves here may be up to a kilometer long, but only experienced surfers should attempt them.

Salsa brava (Puerto Viejo, Caribbean Coast)

Salsa Brava is a top surf destination in the Caribbean due to its strong and hollow waves. It is recommended for expert surfers because of its reef break and powerful currents.

Tips For Surfing in Costa Rica

Respect the Locals: Always show respect for local surfers and adhere to surfing etiquette.

Check the prediction: Keep an eye on the surf prediction and tide charts to determine the optimum conditions.

Safety first: Be wary of rip currents and always surf within your limits. Wearing a leash and choosing a board with a soft top can help improve safety, especially for beginners.

Protect the Environment: Use reef-safe sunscreen and leave no garbage on the beach.

Zip Through the Sky: Canopy Tours

Canopy excursions provide an exciting opportunity to see Costa Rica's magnificent jungles and rich animals from above. These trips entail moving from platform to platform high above the forest floor using a network of zip wires. Here are some of the best places for canopy tours in Costa Rica:

Monteverde Cloud Forest

Monteverde is a popular destination for canopy tours in Costa Rica, with stunning views of the cloud forest. The region is home to multiple zip line companies, each providing a distinct experience, including the country's longest zip line.

Wildlife: Look for beautiful birds such as the dazzling quetzal and different monkey species.

Arenal Volcano Area

The region around Arenal Volcano has various canopy excursions that provide breathtaking views of the volcano and Lake Arenal. Some trips involve rappelling, Tarzan swings, and hanging bridges.

Wildlife: While zipping over the canopy, you may see toucans, sloths, and howler monkeys.

Manuel Antonio

Canopy excursions in Manuel Antonio sometimes mix zip line with additional activities such as hiking and waterfall rappelling. The coastline scenery and diverse wildlife make it an unforgettable experience.

Wildlife: The rainforest is home to a variety of animals, including white-faced capuchin monkeys and lizards.

Guanacaste

Guanacaste's dry tropical woods and gorgeous beaches provide as a unique setting for canopy excursions. Some trips include ocean views and the opportunity to watch the sunset from the ziplines.

Wildlife: Keep an eye out for colorful birds, and if you're lucky, you could see a howler monkey.

Tips For Canopy Tours

Dress appropriately: long trousers, closed-toe shoes, and a comfortable shirt are encouraged. Avoid wearing loose clothes and jewelry.

Listen To Your Guides: Pay attention during the safety briefing and follow the advice given by your guides.

Check Weight and Age limitations: Most canopy excursions have weight and age limitations to ensure the safety of participants. Check them ahead of time.

Bring a Camera: If you wish to document your experience, make sure your camera or phone is securely linked to you.

Stay Calm: If you're terrified of heights, take deep breaths and concentrate on the stunning scenery to calm your anxiety.

Wildlife Watching: Meeting the Locals

Costa Rica is a wildlife enthusiast's paradise, with its abundant biodiversity and protected areas offering several opportunity to watch a diverse range of creatures in their natural settings. Here are some of the best sites and suggestions for wildlife watching in this wonderful country:

Corcovado National Park (the Osa Peninsula)
Highlights: Corcovado is regarded as one of the most biodiverse areas on Earth, including uncommon species like as Baird's tapirs, jaguars, and the endangered scarlet macaw.

The best time to visit is during the dry season (December to April), when the paths are simpler to navigate.

Tortuguero National Park (the Caribbean Coast)

Highlights: Known for its sea turtle breeding beaches, particularly for green turtles. The park's waterways are also ideal for observing caimans, manatees, and many bird species.

Best time to visit: July to October, when turtles nest.

Monteverde Cloud Forest Reserve

Highlights: Known for its magnificent quetzals, hummingbirds, and other cloud forest wildlife. The lush vegetation and colder temperatures provide a distinct environment for fauna.

The best time to visit is between March and July, when the quetzals are breeding.

Manuel Antonio National Park

Highlights: One of Costa Rica's most popular parks, famous for its stunning beaches and abundant wildlife, which includes sloths, white-faced capuchin monkeys, and hundreds of other bird species.

The best time to visit is during the dry season (December to April), which offers better animal visibility and park accessibility.

Cano Negro Wildlife Refuge

Highlights: A wetland reserve with a diverse range of bird species, including the Jabiru stork, caimans, turtles, and freshwater fish.

The best time to visit is during the wet season (May to November), when the lagoons and rivers are full and attract more species.

Tips for Wildlife Watching:
Hire a Guide: Local guides are knowledgeable about the area's wildlife and can help you locate and identify species that you would otherwise miss.
Be Patient and Quiet: Being quiet and patient increases your chances of seeing wildlife. Avoid loud noises and quick movements.
Use Binoculars: A decent set of binoculars is required to see birds and animals in the distance.
Respect Nature: Keep a safe distance from wildlife, do not feed the animals, and adhere to all park laws and regulations.
Be prepared: Pack bug repellant, sunscreen, water, and snacks. Wear hiking-appropriate clothing and footwear, as well as protective gear.

WHERE TO STAY:
ACCOMMODATIONS FOR ALL

Luxury Resorts: Indulging in Comfort

Costa Rica has a variety of lodgings to fit any traveler's needs and budget. Here are some possibilities for your accommodation, ranging from eco-friendly cottages to opulent resorts.

Four Seasons Resort Costa Rica at Peninsula Papagayo (Guanacaste):

Description: This upmarket resort on the Pacific coast features beautiful ocean views, various pools, a world-class spa, and access to two private beaches.

Activities include golfing on the Arnold Palmer-designed course, water activities, and guided nature treks.

Tabacón Thermal Resort and Spa (Arenal):

This luxurious resort, known for its natural hot springs and beautiful tropical gardens, offers a peaceful retreat near the Arenal Volcano.

Activities include soaking in hot pools, receiving spa treatments, and visiting the adjacent Arenal Volcano National Park.

🏠 Nayara Spring (Arenal):

An adults-only boutique resort noted for its individual villas with plunge pools fed by natural hot springs, nestled in the jungle.

Activities include yoga lessons, massage treatments, and bird-watching expeditions.

🏠 The Springs Resort & Spa in Arenal:

This resort offers panoramic views of the Arenal Volcano and includes hot springs, a wildlife refuge, and elegant apartments.

Activities include river tubing, horseback riding, and visiting the on-site animal refuge.

🏠 JW Marriott Guanacaste Resort and Spa (Guanacaste):

This resort, located on a quiet beach, features a huge pool, a spa, and magnificent suites with balcony views.

Activities include surfing instruction, snorkeling, and golfing at the adjacent Hacienda Pinilla Golf Course.

Tips for Staying at Luxury Resorts:

plan in Advance: Luxury resorts fill up quickly, especially during peak season, so it's best to plan your stay ahead of time.

Check for Packages: Many resorts offer packages that include meals, activities, and spa treatments, which can add value.

Dress Code: Some resorts may have dress rules for specific areas or activities, so bring suitable clothes.

Eco-Lodges: Sleeping Green

Eco-lodges in Costa Rica are ideal for those who wish to immerse themselves in nature while reducing their environmental effect. These lodgings prioritize sustainability, conservation, and giving visitors with a true connection to the natural world. Here are some noteworthy eco-lodges:

🏠 **Lapa Rios Lodge (the Osa Peninsula):**

Lapa Rios Lodge, located in a private natural reserve in the southern rainforest, is a pioneering example of sustainable tourism. The resort provides magnificent bungalows with stunning ocean views and is dedicated to preserving the surrounding species.

Activities include rainforest walks, bird viewing, and sustainable excursions such as the "Twigs, Pigs, and Garbage" tour.

Finca Rosa Blanca Coffee Plantation & Inn, Heredia:

Description: This boutique hotel is located in the middle highlands on a thriving coffee farm. It is renowned for its distinctive architecture, organic coffee, and dedication to sustainability.

Activities include coffee plantation trips, bird viewing, and cultural visits of local communities.

Pacuare Lodge, Turrialba:

Pacuare Lodge, located in the jungle along the Pacuare River, is only accessible by raft or 4x4. The resort provides luxurious thatched-roof bungalows and is committed to environmental and social responsibility.

Activities include whitewater rafting, canopy excursions, and indigenous cultural experiences.

Tortuga Lodge & Gardens (Tortugueros):

Description: Located in the isolated Tortuguero National Park, this eco-lodge provides comfortable lodgings with river views and is an excellent location for animal viewing, particularly sea turtles.

Activities include guided boat cruises, kayaking, and turtle nesting tours (seasonal).

Monteverde Lodge and Gardens (Monteverde)

This eco-lodge, nestled in the cloud forest, boasts stunning gardens, a butterfly garden, and snug rooms with forest views. It is dedicated to ecological principles and provides a tranquil refuge in the highlands.

Activities include guided cloud forest treks, bird-watching, and excursions to surrounding reserves and sites.

Tips for Staying in Eco-Lodges

Book Directly: Booking directly with the resort can frequently result in lower prices and more money going towards conservation initiatives.

Pack responsibly: Bring environmentally friendly toiletries and reusable water bottles to help decrease plastic waste.

Respect the environment. Follow the lodge's suggestions to reduce your environmental effect, such as saving water and electricity.

Budget-Friendly: Hostels and Guesthouses

Costa Rica has a variety of low-cost lodgings, including hostels and guesthouses, that offer a pleasant and economical way to see the country.

These alternatives are ideal for backpackers, lone travelers, and anybody trying to maximize their trip budget. Here are some recommendations and popular areas for seeking affordable stays:

Popular Budget Friendly Destinations:

San José
Hostel Urbano: This hostel, located in the popular San Pedro district, offers a sociable environment as well as dormitories and private rooms.
Costa Rica Guesthouse: A lovely guesthouse in a colonial-style property that provides individual rooms with a pleasant and homely atmosphere.

La Fortuna (Arenal Volcanic Area)
Arenal Backpackers Resort: This hostel has a pool, an on-site bar, and both dormitory and private tent accommodations, all with views of the Arenal Volcano.
La Choza Inn Hostel is a family-run hostel with a welcoming ambiance that offers individual rooms, dormitories, and a community kitchen.

Monteverde
Camino Verde Hostel: This hostel is known for its helpful staff and excellent accommodations, which include a combination of dormitories and private

rooms, as well as a communal kitchen and common spaces.

Cabinas El Pueblo is a pleasant guesthouse with a family-like environment that offers individual rooms and dormitories as well as complimentary breakfast.

Tamarindo (Guanacaste)

Selina Tamarindo: Part of the acclaimed Selina brand, this hostel has a lively environment, a pool, a coworking area, and a variety of lodging options.

Pura Vida Hostel: A laid-back hostel with a mix of dormitories and private rooms that is just a short walk from the beach.

Tips for staying in hostels and guesthouses

Book in Advance: Budget lodgings fill up fast, especially during peak season, so it's best to book ahead of time.

Check reviews: Read other guests' reviews to get a feel for the hostel or guesthouse's environment, cleanliness, and facilities.

Pack a padlock: While many hostels have lockers for valuables, you will likcly need to bring your own padlock.

Be Social: Hostels are excellent places to meet other travelers, so don't be hesitant about striking up a discussion in the common areas.

Unique Stays: Treehouses and Glamping

Costa Rica has a range of unusual hotel options, including treehouses and glamping locations. These lodgings provide a combination of adventure and comfort, allowing you to immerse yourself in nature while yet enjoying contemporary comforts.

Treehouses

Tree House Lodge, Puerto Viejo:
Description: This resort, located on a private seaside property, provides many treehouse alternatives, including one built around a 100-year-old Sangrillo tree. It's an environmentally friendly hideaway with access to stunning beaches and lush woods.
Activities include snorkeling, canoeing, and visiting the neighboring Gandoca-Manzanillo Wildlife Refuge.

Finca Bella Vista Treehouse Community (South Pacific):
A sustainable treehouse village located in the jungle canopy. Each treehouse is unique, providing breathtaking vistas and an authentic off-grid experience.
Activities include hiking, zip-lining, and bird viewing.
Glamping:

Rafiki Safari Lodge, Savegre River Valley:
This luxurious tent camp is located on a private reserve and features huge safari-style tents with private toilets and balconies that overlook the river.
Activities include whitewater rafting, horseback riding, and guided nature treks.

Glamping Costa Rica (La Fortuna):
Description: This glamping resort near the Arenal Volcano provides cozy tents with individual toilets and breathtaking views of the surrounding countryside.
Activities include hot springs, zip line, and visiting Arenal Volcano National Park.

Tips for a Unique Stay:
Book Early: Treehouses and glamping sites are frequently restricted in quantity and can sell out fast, especially during peak season.
prepare Appropriately: While these amenities provide luxury, it is critical to prepare for the outdoors, including bug repellant and sturdy footwear.
Embrace the Experience: Unique stays frequently give an opportunity to detach from technology and reconnect with nature. Enjoy the quiet and beauty of your surroundings.

GETTING AROUND: TRAVELING WITHIN COSTA RICA

Public Transport: Buses and Shuttles

Costa Rica has a variety of transportation alternatives to accommodate different travel types and budgets. Here's a guide to help you go about the country:

Public transportation: Buses and Shuttles

Buses

Buses are the most cost-effective mode of transportation in Costa Rica, connecting cities and communities. Fares are very priced, making this a popular choice for budget tourists.

Coverage: Costa Rica's bus system is comprehensive, with lines linking major towns, tourist attractions, and isolated places.

Buses to prominent places operate often, however timetables in outlying areas may vary. It is best to verify the schedule in advance.

Tips: Be prepared for lengthier journey times because buses frequently make many stops. Keep a watch on your valuables, particularly on crowded buses.

Shuttles

Convenience: Shuttle services are more comfortable and convenient than public buses. They offer door-to-door service between hotels and popular tourist attractions.

Shuttles cost more than public buses, but they are still inexpensive, especially given the increased convenience.

Booking: It is best to reserve shuttle services in advance, especially during high travel seasons.

Shared versus Private: You have the option of using shared shuttles, which are less expensive, or private shuttles, which provide greater schedule and route flexibility.

Tips for using public transportation:

Plan: Look into routes and timetables ahead of time, especially if you're going to a less popular destination.

Be flexible: Prepare for delays or changes in timetables, which might occur due to weather or road conditions.

Learn basic Spanish: Knowing a few basic Spanish words will help you navigate the bus system and communicate with drivers.

Have a Small Change: It's a good idea to have small banknotes and coins on hand when paying for bus fares because drivers may not have change for larger notes.

Renting a Car: Tips for the Road

Renting a car in Costa Rica allows you to explore at your own leisure and see off-the-beaten-path attractions. Here are some suggestions for a smooth driving experience:

Choose the Right Vehicle: Depending on your schedule, you should consider hiring a 4x4 or SUV, especially if you want to visit rural regions or national parks with dirt roads.

Insurance: Make sure you understand your insurance alternatives and obligations. Costa Rica requires minimum insurance, however extra coverage is suggested for peace of mind.

Driving Conditions: Be prepared for a variety of road conditions, including narrow roads, potholes, and some unpaved sections. Drive slowly, particularly in hilly locations and during the rainy season.

Navigation requires GPS or a dependable map app, as road signs might be minimal. If you have limited cell service, download offline maps.

Traffic Laws: Follow speed limits, use seat belts, and refrain from using your phone while driving. Be advised that Costa Rica has stringent drunk driving regulations.

Parking: Use secured parking lots in tourist areas when available. Never leave any valuables exposed in your automobile.

Domestic flights: Hopping between destinations

Domestic flights are a useful alternative for people with limited time or who need to travel great distances. Costa Rica has various regional airports, making it easier to travel between destinations:

The main domestic airlines are Sansa Airlines and Skyway, which fly to Liberia, Tambor, Quepos, and Tortuguero.

Booking: Book flights in early, especially during peak season, since seats fill up rapidly.

luggage: Check the luggage allotment and surcharges, as smaller flights have tighter weight restrictions.

Timing: Domestic flights may save you a lot of time compared to driving or taking busses, allowing you to make the most of your time in each destination.

ITINERARIES: 7 DAYS IN PARADISE

For Nature Lovers: Rainforests and Wildlife

🌲 **Day 1: Arrival in San José**
Arrive at the Juan Santamaría International Airport.
Transfer to your accommodation in San José and unwind after your adventure.
Eat a classic Costa Rican supper at a local restaurant.

🌲 **Day 2: Braulio Carrillo National Park, Tortuguero**
Depart early for Braulio Carrillo National Park, where you may enjoy a magnificent aerial tram ride over the rainforest canopy.
Continue to Tortuguero National Park, where you will arrive by boat via the canals to your resort.
In the evening, go on a guided stroll to learn about the area's nocturnal animals.

🌲 **Day 3: Tortuguero National Park.**
Take a morning boat cruise to see animals including monkeys, toucans, and caimans.
Visit the Sea Turtle Conservancy to learn more about sea turtle conservation initiatives.

Optional: If you visit during turtle nesting season (July-October), take a night cruise to see sea turtles depositing eggs on the beach.

 Day 4: Tortuguero to Arenal

Depart Tortuguero and proceed to La Fortuna, home of the Arenal Volcano.

Check into your accommodation and spend the day at leisure, possibly visiting a hot springs resort to soak in the thermal waters.

 Day 5 - Arenal Volcano National Park

A guided trip in Arenal Volcano National Park provides views of the volcano and the surrounding jungle.

In the afternoon, take a walk among the treetops at Mistico Arenal Hanging Bridges Park.

Optional: Take a wildlife viewing night excursion through the rainforest.

 Day 6: Arenal to Monteverde

Travel to Monteverde, which is noted for its cloud forests.

Take a guided tour through the Monteverde Cloud Forest Reserve to witness the dazzling quetzal and other unusual species.

In the evening, explore Santa Elena by visiting local eateries and cafés.

Day 7: Monteverde to San José

Spend the morning at a coffee farm, learning about coffee production and sampling freshly brewed Costa Rican coffee.

Return to San Jose in the afternoon.

Before leaving, treat yourself to a last supper or explore the city's nightlife.

 Day 8: Departure

Transfer to the airport for your trip home, bringing with you memories of Costa Rica's breathtaking natural beauty and animals.

For Beach Bums: Sun, Sand, and Surf

 Day 1: Arrival in San Jose

Arrive at the Juan Santamaría International Airport.

Transfer to your accommodation in San José and unwind after your adventure.

Have a quiet meal at a local restaurant or discover the city's nightlife.

 Day 2: San José to Manuel Antonio.

Depart early for Manuel Antonio, which is famed for its stunning beaches and national park.

Check in to your beachfront hotel and spend the day lounging on the beach.

A neighborhood restaurant offers a sunset supper with coastal views.

Day 3: Manuel Antonio National Park

Visit Manuel Antonio National Park for a guided trip to see sloths, monkeys, and colorful birds.

Spend the remainder of the day relaxing on the park's gorgeous beaches or participating in water sports such as snorkeling or paddleboarding.

Day 4 - Manuel Antonio to Santa Teresa

Travel to Santa Teresa, a relaxed surf town on the Nicoya Peninsula.

Check into your lodging and explore the town's beautiful beaches and surf locations.

Watch the sunset from the beach and have a leisurely meal at a beachfront café.

Day 5: Surfing in Santa Teresa

Take a surf lesson or hire a board and spend the day surfing.

Relax on the beach or go to a nearby yoga school for a restorative lesson.

A neighborhood eatery serves fresh fish for supper.

Day 6 - Santa Teresa to Tamarindo

Visit Tamarindo, another famous surf location with a vibrant beach atmosphere.

Spend the afternoon surfing, sunbathing, or visiting the town's shops and eateries.

A visit to a seaside bar or club allows you to experience Tamarindo's bustling nightlife.

 Day 7: Tamarindo Beach Day.

Spend the entire day at the beach, exploring different surf breaks or taking a catamaran cruise for snorkeling and sunset views.

Celebrate your final evening with a seaside BBQ or a fancy dining experience in town.

 Day 8: Departure

Return to San José for your trip home, carrying with you memories of Costa Rica's beautiful beaches and surfing culture.

For Culture Enthusiasts: Cities and Traditions

Day 1: Arrival in San José

Arrive at the Juan Santamaría International Airport.

Transfer to your accommodation in San José and unwind after your adventure.

Explore the city's cultural icons, including the National Theatre and the Gold Museum.

Day 2: San José to Cartago

Visit the Basilica of Our Lady of the Angels in Cartago, which is an important religious and historical landmark.

Discover the remains of the Santiago Apóstol Parish and the Lankester Botanical Gardens.

Return to San José and eat a traditional Costa Rican supper at a nearby restaurant.

 Day 3: San José - Sarchí and Zarcero.

Visit Sarchí, noted for its colorful oxcarts and artisan products. Visit a local workshop to learn the ancient technique of oxcart painting.

Continue to Zarcero to view the unique topiary garden in front of the church.

Return to San Jose in the evening.

 Day 4: San José to Guanacaste

Travel to Guanacaste, a region known for its cowboy culture, traditional music, and dancing.

Visit a functioning hacienda to learn about traditional ranch life and have a typical Guanacaste meal.

After checking into your accommodation, spend the evening relaxing on the beach.

 Day 5: Guanacaste to Monteverde

Travel to Monteverde, a cloud forest region famed for producing coffee and cheese.

Visit a coffee plantation to learn about the production process and try some local brews.

In the evening, take a night stroll in the cloud forest or watch a cultural show.

🌲 Day 6: Monteverde to La Fortuna

Explore the Monteverde Cloud Forest Reserve, which is home to a varied range of plants and animals.

Travel to La Fortuna, near the Arenal Volcano. Visit a nearby hot spring and soak in the thermal waters.

Enjoy a classic Costa Rican supper with a view of the volcano.

🌲 Day 7: La Fortuna to San José.

Visit Arenal Volcano National Park for a guided trek to learn about the volcanic activity and natural history.

Return to San José and spend your final evening exploring the city's lively nightlife or having a goodbye meal.

🌲 Day 8: Departure

Transfer to the airport for your trip home, bringing with you memories of Costa Rica's vibrant culture and customs.

Rio Celeste

Traveling Responsibly: Sustainable Tourism

Costa Rica is a leader in sustainable tourism, and traveling wisely is an important aspect of enjoying the nation. Here are some suggestions for helping local people and practicing sustainable tourism:

Supporting Local Communities: Where to Shop and Eat

Shop Locally
Visit local markets and artisan cooperatives to buy handcrafted goods, fabrics, and souvenirs. This not only benefits local artists, but also helps to maintain old skills.
Farmers' markets, also known as "ferias" in Costa Rica, are where you can buy fresh vegetables and locally made items. This benefits local farmers while also reducing the carbon impact of goods transportation.

Eat Locally
Local Eateries: Visit "sodas," tiny family-owned eateries that provide authentic Costa Rican cuisine.

This is an excellent chance to sample genuine food while supporting local companies.

Farm-to-Table: Look for restaurants that use locally sourced food and promote farm-to-table dining. This promotes local agriculture while reducing the environmental effect of food transportation.

Community-based tourism

Participate in community-based tourism activities such as visiting indigenous villages, attending cultural seminars, or staying at locally owned lodges. These interactions foster a better knowledge of local culture and directly help communities.

Volunteer Opportunities

During your visit, consider working for local groups or environmental initiatives. This may be a satisfying way to give back and help with sustainable development.

Additional Tips for Sustainable Tourism

Conserve Resources: Be cautious of your water and energy consumption, particularly in locations with limited resources. Turn off the lights and air conditioning when not in use, and take brief showers.

Reduce Waste: Carry a reusable water bottle, shopping bags, and utensils to cut down on single-use plastics. Dispose of rubbish appropriately and recycle wherever feasible.

Respect Wildlife: Keep a safe distance from wildlife, do not feed animals, and avoid purchasing items from endangered species.
Choose Eco-Friendly Activities: Select activities that have a low environmental effect, such as hiking, kayaking, and bird watching.

Eco-Friendly Practices: Leaving a Light Footprint

Adopting eco-friendly behaviors when traveling in Costa Rica not only benefits the environment, but also improves your whole experience. Here are some tips to leave a minimal footprint:

Reduce energy consumption
Unplug items: To save energy, unplug chargers and electronic devices while they are not in use.
Use Natural Light: Make the most of natural sunshine and switch off lights when you leave the room.
Choose eco-friendly accommodations. Choose hotels or lodges that utilize renewable energy and use energy-saving strategies.

Conserve water
Take Shorter Showers: To save water, limit your shower time.

Reuse Towels: Instead of asking new towels every day, hang them up to dry and reuse.

Report Leaks: Please notify your accommodation if you see any leaky faucets or toilets.

Minimize waste

Bring a Reusable Water Bottle: Refill your bottle rather than purchasing single-use plastic bottles. Most hotels and restaurants provide clean drinking water.

Say no to single-use plastics. Avoid using plastic straws, utensils, and bags. Bring your own reusable alternatives.

Recycle: Place recyclable materials such as plastic, glass, and paper in designated recycling containers.

Respect nature

Stay on routes: When trekking, use defined routes to prevent hurting delicate ecosystems.

Leave No Trace: Take all garbage with you and leave natural environments just as you found them.

Avoid Disturbing Wildlife: Keep a safe distance from animals and refrain from making loud noises that may disturb them.

Support Sustainable Activities

Choose Eco-Friendly Tours: Look for tours and activities that have a low environmental effect and promote conservation.

Buy Local and Sustainable things: Look for things created locally and sustainably, such organic coffee or chocolate.

Educate Yourself and Others: Discover the local environment and share your expertise with other tourists.

Wildlife Conservation: Respecting Nature

Costa Rica is well-known for its abundant biodiversity and commitment to conservation. As a tourist, you can help safeguard the animals and natural environments. Here are some recommendations for appreciating environment and helping to save wildlife:

Observe Wildlife Responsibly

Maintain a Safe Distance: Always keep a respectful distance from animals to prevent stressing them or disrupting their natural behavior.

Never feed wild animals since it might lead to dependence on people, health issues, and hostile behavior.

Quiet Observation: Keep your noise levels low to prevent upsetting the animals. Use binoculars or a zoom lens to get a better look without going too near.

Support Protected Areas

Visit National Parks and Reserves: Entrance fees to protected places help to fund conservation efforts and ensure the survival of these critical ecosystems.

Follow Park Rules: Comply with all rules and restrictions, such as keeping on authorized pathways and not disturbing any natural items.

Choose Environmentally Friendly Tours

Select Responsible Operators. Choose tour firms and operators that promote ethical wildlife watching and conservation projects.

Participate in conservation activities. Look for ways to participate in activities such as reforestation initiatives, beach cleanups, and turtle protection programs.

Minimize Your Impact

Pack In, Pack Out: Take all of your rubbish with you and dispose of it correctly. Leave natural areas as clean as you found them.

Use environmentally friendly products: Choose biodegradable sunscreen and insect repellant to prevent contaminating water sources and endangering marine life.

Promote conservation awareness
Educate Yourself and Others: Learn about local species and habitats, then share your knowledge with others to improve conservation awareness.
Support conservation organizations. Consider giving or volunteering for Costa Rican animal conservation groups.

USEFUL INFORMATION: TIPS AND RESOURCES

Health and Safety: Staying Well in Costa Rica

Costa Rica is typically a secure and healthy place, but you must take some steps to have a worry-free trip. Here are some health and safety guidelines:

Health:
immunizations: Ensure that you are up to date on standard immunizations. Depending on your travel intentions, you may additionally require immunizations against hepatitis A, typhoid, or yellow fever. Consult your healthcare physician or a travel clinic.
Purchase comprehensive travel insurance that covers medical situations including evacuation and hospitalization.
Water Safety: Tap water is typically safe to drink in Costa Rica, particularly in cities. However, if you are in a rural area, it is safer to consume bottled or filtered water.
Food Safety: Enjoy the local cuisine, but be wary of street food and undercooked meals. Make careful to wash fruits and vegetables with clean water.

Insect Protection: Use insect repellent and long-sleeved clothes to avoid mosquito-borne infections such as dengue and Zika.

Sun Protection: Use sunscreen on a regular basis, wear a helmet, and remain hydrated to avoid sunburn and heatstroke.

Safety:

Crime: Although Costa Rica is mostly secure, small crime can occur. Be cautious in crowded areas, avoid wandering alone at night, and keep valuables safe.

Road Safety: When driving, be alert of hazardous road conditions and unpredictable driving behavior. Always wear a seatbelt and avoid driving at night.

Natural hazards: Costa Rica is prone to earthquakes and volcanic activity. Familiarize yourself with safety protocols in case of such an incident.

Emergency Numbers: Maintain a list of emergency contacts, such as the local police (911), medical services, and your country's embassy or consulate.

Additional Tips:

Language: While many Costa Ricans speak English, particularly in tourist regions, knowing some basic Spanish phrases might be beneficial.

Currency: The Costa Rican colón (CRC) is the official currency, however US dollars are often accepted. Always keep a little amount of local cash on hand.

Cultural Respect: Costa Ricans, sometimes known as "Ticos," are recognized for being kind. Respect local customs, dress appropriately while visiting holy places, and always obtain permission before photographing people.

Money Matters: Currency and Budgeting

Costa Rica's currency is the Costa Rican colón (CRC), however US dollars are often accepted, particularly in tourist destinations. Here are some ideas for managing your funds while visiting Costa Rica:

Check the currency rate before your journey. While US dollars are accepted, paying in colones frequently results in a better value for minor goods.

Credit Cards and ATMs: Major credit cards are accepted in most hotels, restaurants, and major stores. ATMs are readily available, although it is advisable to carry some cash for little transactions especially in remote regions.

Budgeting: Costa Rica may be as pricey or as affordable as you like. Prices for accommodation, food, and activities vary, so plan accordingly. Hostels, local cafes, and public transit are excellent money-saving options.

Tipping: A 10% service fee is frequently added to restaurant bills. It is usual to provide a tiny extra tip (about 5%) for good service. Tipping is not required in taxis, however, rounding up the fare is appreciated.

Staying Connected with the Internet and Phones

Staying connected in Costa Rica is very simple, with decent internet and mobile phone service in most regions.

Wi-Fi: Most hotels, restaurants, and cafés have free Wi-Fi. The connection may be slower in isolated locations, but it is usually dependable in cities and tourist destinations.

SIM Cards: If you require a local phone number or a data plan, getting a prepaid SIM card is a simple choice. They're available in airports and stores and work with unlocked phones. Kolbi, Movistar, and Claro are prominent providers.

International Calling: Ask your cellphone operator about international roaming rates. Alternatively, utilize Wi-Fi-enabled programs such as WhatsApp, Skype, or Zoom.

Emergency Numbers: Keep critical contact information handy, such as local emergency services (911), your embassy, and home connections.

FINAL THOUGHTS: EMBRACING PURA VIDA

As your time in Costa Rica comes to an end, take a minute to reflect on the experiences and memories you've made. Embracing the notion of "Pura Vida," or "pure life," entails more than just admiring the country's natural beauty; it entails cultivating an attitude of appreciation, attentiveness, and joy in the basic joys of living.

Reflecting on your journey

Nature's Wonders: Reflect on the many settings you've seen, from lush rainforests and beautiful beaches to magnificent volcanoes and tranquil cloud forests. Consider how these natural wonders have influenced your respect for the environment and the value of conservation.

Cultural Connections: Think about your relationships with the people, the traditional foods you've had, and the cultural events you've seen. These encounters have most likely produced a better knowledge of Costa Rican culture and the friendliness of its people.

Adventure and Relaxation: Whether you've been zip-lining through the canopy, surfing the waves, or simply relaxing in a hot spring, remember the moments of excitement and peace that defined your vacation.

Personal Growth: Think about how this adventure has improved your life, whether it's via new connections, conquering obstacles, or obtaining a new perspective on what's important to you.

Embracing Pura Vida outside Costa Rica

As you return home, consider how you may bring the essence of Pura Vida into your daily life. This might be spending time to enjoy nature, connecting with others around you, or finding joy in life's little moments. The spirit of Pura Vida reminds us that, no matter where we are, we may choose to live a life of appreciation, generosity, and amazement.

Visitors to Costa Rica are left with a lasting impression of the country's natural beauty, vibrant culture, and Pura Vida attitude. Take this experience with you and let it motivate you to live a life full of experiences, relationships, and gratitude for the world around you.

Saying Goodbye: Until Next Time

Leaving Costa Rica might be sad, but the memories and experiences you have will stay with you long after you return home. As you prepare to say farewell, take a time to enjoy your last hours in this wonderful country:

Last Moments: Spend your final day revisiting a favorite location or resting in a serene atmosphere. Enjoy a farewell supper of Costa Rican cuisine and celebrate your travels with a cool tropical cocktail.

Gratitude: Take the time to thank everyone who helped make your vacation memorable, whether it was the hotel staff, tour guides, or new friends you made along the route.

keepsakes: Get a few last-minute keepsakes to remember your time in Costa Rica. Whether it's a piece of local art, a bag of coffee, or a handcrafted craft, these objects will help you remember.

Reflection: As you depart, consider the highlights of your vacation and how it has enhanced your life. Consider what you've learnt and how you've developed from this experience.

Until Next Time:

Stay Connected: Stay in contact with the people you've met and follow local companies or groups on social media to stay up to speed on what's going on in Costa Rica.

Plan your return: If Costa Rica has won your heart, consider when you could return. There's always more to discover, from secluded beaches to unexplored woods.

Share your story: Share your experiences with friends and family, and inspire others to visit Costa Rica and experience its natural beauty and friendliness. Your tales and suggestions may inspire future travelers.

Saying farewell to Costa Rica does not have to mean the end. It's simply a "hasta luego" (see you later) as you carry the spirit of Pura Vida with you and anticipate the day when you may return to this lovely nation. Until the next time, Costa Rica will have a particular place in your heart, ready for you to return and discover even more of its natural beauties and cultural riches.

Appendix: Handy References

Emergency Contacts: Staying Safe

It's important to have a list of emergency contacts while traveling in Costa Rica to ensure your safety and well-being. Here are some essential numbers and contacts to keep handy:

Emergency Services:
General Emergency: 911 (Ambulance, Fire, Police)
Red Cross (Cruz Roja): 128
Roadside Assistance (MOPT): 800-872-6748 or 800-TRANSITO

Medical Services:
Hospital México (San José): +506 2242-6700
Hospital CIMA (San José/Escazú): +506 2208-1000
Hospital Clínica Bíblica (San José): +506 2522-1000
Hospital La Católica (San José/Guadalupe): +506 2246-3000

Embassies and Consulates:
U.S. Embassy in San José: +506 2519-2000
Canadian Embassy in San José: +506 2242-4400
British Embassy in San José: +506 2258-2025
Australian Embassy in Mexico City (serving Costa Rica): +52 55 1101 2200

Tourist Assistance:

Instituto Costarricense de Turismo (ICT) - Tourist Information: +506 2299-5800
Tourist Police: +506 2586-4287

Other Useful Contacts:

Road Conditions and Traffic Information: 800-872-6748 or 800-TRANSITO
Directory Assistance: 1113 (Spanish), 1114 (English)

Tips for Staying Safe:

Keep a Physical Copy: Have a printed copy of these contacts in case your phone is lost or out of battery.

Program Numbers into Your Phone: Save these numbers in your phone for quick access.

Inform Others: Let your hotel or local contacts know your whereabouts, especially if you're venturing into remote areas.

Travel Insurance: Ensure you have comprehensive travel insurance that covers medical emergencies and evacuation.

COSTA RICA TRAVEL BUDGET PLANNER

DESTINATION			TRAVEL DATES	

TRANSPORTATION			ACTIVITIES		
expenses	budget	actual	expenses	budget	actual
Total:			Total:		

ACCOMMODATION			PRE-TRIP EXPENSES		
expenses	budget	actual	expenses	budget	actual
Total:			Total:		

FOOD & DRINK			OTHER		
expenses	budget	actual	expenses	budget	actual
Total:			Total:		

NOTES	GRAND TOTAL	budget	actual

COSTA RICA TRAVEL BUDGET PLANNER

DESTINATION			TRAVEL DATES		

TRANSPORTATION			ACTIVITIES		
expenses	budget	actual	expenses	budget	actual
Total:			Total:		

ACCOMMODATION			PRE-TRIP EXPENSES		
expenses	budget	actual	expenses	budget	actual
Total:			Total:		

FOOD & DRINK			OTHER		
expenses	budget	actual	expenses	budget	actual
Total:			Total:		

NOTES

GRAND TOTAL	budget	actual

COSTA RICA TRAVEL BUDGET PLANNER

| DESTINATION | | TRAVEL DATES | |

TRANSPORTATION

expenses	budget	actual
Total:		

ACTIVITIES

expenses	budget	actual
Total:		

ACCOMMODATION

expenses	budget	actual
Total:		

PRE-TRIP EXPENSES

expenses	budget	actual
Total:		

FOOD & DRINK

expenses	budget	actual
Total:		

OTHER

expenses	budget	actual
Total:		

NOTES

GRAND TOTAL	budget	actual

COSTA RICA TRAVEL BUDGET PLANNER

DESTINATION		TRAVEL DATES	

TRANSPORTATION

expenses	budget	actual
Total:		

ACTIVITIES

expenses	budget	actual
Total:		

ACCOMMODATION

expenses	budget	actual
Total:		

PRE-TRIP EXPENSES

expenses	budget	actual
Total:		

FOOD & DRINK

expenses	budget	actual
Total:		

OTHER

expenses	budget	actual
Total:		

NOTES

GRAND TOTAL	budget	actual

COSTA RICA TRAVEL BUDGET PLANNER

DESTINATION				TRAVEL DATES		

TRANSPORTATION				ACTIVITIES		
expenses	budget	actual		expenses	budget	actual
Total:				Total:		

ACCOMMODATION				PRE-TRIP EXPENSES		
expenses	budget	actual		expenses	budget	actual
Total:				Total:		

FOOD & DRINK				OTHER		
expenses	budget	actual		expenses	budget	actual
Total:				Total:		

NOTES		GRAND TOTAL	budget	actual

COSTA RICA TRAVEL BUDGET PLANNER

DESTINATION		TRAVEL DATES	

TRANSPORTATION

expenses	budget	actual
Total:		

ACTIVITIES

expenses	budget	actual
Total:		

ACCOMMODATION

expenses	budget	actual
Total:		

PRE-TRIP EXPENSES

expenses	budget	actual
Total:		

FOOD & DRINK

expenses	budget	actual
Total:		

OTHER

expenses	budget	actual
Total:		

NOTES

GRAND TOTAL	budget	actual

COSTA RICA TRAVEL BUDGET PLANNER

| DESTINATION | | TRAVEL DATES | |

TRANSPORTATION		
expenses	budget	actual
Total:		

ACTIVITIES		
expenses	budget	actual
Total:		

ACCOMMODATION		
expenses	budget	actual
Total:		

PRE-TRIP EXPENSES		
expenses	budget	actual
Total:		

FOOD & DRINK		
expenses	budget	actual
Total:		

OTHER		
expenses	budget	actual
Total:		

NOTES

GRAND TOTAL	budget	actual

COSTA RICA TRAVEL BUDGET PLANNER

| DESTINATION | | TRAVEL DATES | |

TRANSPORTATION

expenses	budget	actual
Total:		

ACTIVITIES

expenses	budget	actual
Total:		

ACCOMMODATION

expenses	budget	actual
Total:		

PRE-TRIP EXPENSES

expenses	budget	actual
Total:		

FOOD & DRINK

expenses	budget	actual
Total:		

OTHER

expenses	budget	actual
Total:		

NOTES

GRAND TOTAL	budget	actual

COSTA RICA TRAVEL BUDGET PLANNER

| DESTINATION | | TRAVEL DATES | |

TRANSPORTATION		
expenses	budget	actual
Total:		

ACTIVITIES		
expenses	budget	actual
Total:		

ACCOMMODATION		
expenses	budget	actual
Total:		

PRE-TRIP EXPENSES		
expenses	budget	actual
Total:		

FOOD & DRINK		
expenses	budget	actual
Total:		

OTHER		
expenses	budget	actual
Total:		

NOTES

GRAND TOTAL	budget	actual

COSTA RICA TRAVEL BUDGET PLANNER

DESTINATION		TRAVEL DATES	

TRANSPORTATION		
expenses	budget	actual
Total:		

ACTIVITIES		
expenses	budget	actual
Total:		

ACCOMMODATION		
expenses	budget	actual
Total:		

PRE-TRIP EXPENSES		
expenses	budget	actual
Total:		

FOOD & DRINK		
expenses	budget	actual
Total:		

OTHER		
expenses	budget	actual
Total:		

NOTES

GRAND TOTAL	budget	actual

COSTA RICA TRAVEL BUDGET PLANNER

| DESTINATION | | TRAVEL DATES | |

TRANSPORTATION			ACTIVITIES		
expenses	budget	actual	expenses	budget	actual
Total:			Total:		

ACCOMMODATION			PRE-TRIP EXPENSES		
expenses	budget	actual	expenses	budget	actual
Total:			Total:		

FOOD & DRINK			OTHER		
expenses	budget	actual	expenses	budget	actual
Total:			Total:		

NOTES

GRAND TOTAL	budget	actual

COSTA RICA TRAVEL BUDGET PLANNER

| DESTINATION | | TRAVEL DATES | |

TRANSPORTATION

expenses	budget	actual
Total:		

ACTIVITIES

expenses	budget	actual
Total:		

ACCOMMODATION

expenses	budget	actual
Total:		

PRE-TRIP EXPENSES

expenses	budget	actual
Total:		

FOOD & DRINK

expenses	budget	actual
Total:		

OTHER

expenses	budget	actual
Total:		

NOTES

GRAND TOTAL	budget	actual

COSTA RICA TRAVEL BUDGET PLANNER

| DESTINATION | | TRAVEL DATES | |

TRANSPORTATION		
expenses	budget	actual
Total:		

ACTIVITIES		
expenses	budget	actual
Total:		

ACCOMMODATION		
expenses	budget	actual
Total:		

PRE-TRIP EXPENSES		
expenses	budget	actual
Total:		

FOOD & DRINK		
expenses	budget	actual
Total:		

OTHER		
expenses	budget	actual
Total:		

NOTES

GRAND TOTAL	budget	actual

COSTA RICA TRAVEL BUDGET PLANNER

| DESTINATION | | | TRAVEL DATES | | |

TRANSPORTATION			ACTIVITIES		
expenses	budget	actual	expenses	budget	actual
Total:			Total:		

ACCOMMODATION			PRE-TRIP EXPENSES		
expenses	budget	actual	expenses	budget	actual
Total:			Total:		

FOOD & DRINK			OTHER		
expenses	budget	actual	expenses	budget	actual
Total:			Total:		

NOTES

GRAND TOTAL	budget	actual

Page 162

VISIT COSTA RICA

Made in United States
Orlando, FL
21 November 2024

54222277R00091